The Private Music Instruction Manual

A Guide for the Independent Music Educator

Rebecca Osborn

Printed in Victoria, Canada

A cataloguing record for this book that includes the U.S. Library of Congress Classification number, the Library of Congress Call number and the Dewey Decimal cataloguing code is available from the National Library of Canada. The complete cataloguing record can be obtained from the National Library's online database at: www.nlc-bnc.ca/amicus/index-e.html
ISBN: 1-4120-2531-1

TRAFFORD

This book was published *on-demand* in cooperation with Trafford Publishing.
On-demand publishing is a unique process and service of making a book available for retail sale to the public taking advantage of on-demand manufacturing and Internet marketing..**On-demand publishing** includes promotions, retail sales, manufacturing, order fulfilment, accounting and collecting royalties on behalf of the author.

Suite 6E, 2333 Government St., Victoria, B.C. V8T 4P4, CANADA
Phone   250-383-6864   Toll-free   1-888-232-4444 (Canada & US)
Fax   250-383-6804   E-mail sales@trafford.com
Web site   www.trafford.com   TRAFFORD PUBLISHING IS A DIVISION OF TRAFFORD HOLDINGS LTD.
Trafford Catalogue #04-0359   www.trafford.com/robots/04-0359 .html

10   9   8   7   6   5   4   3   2   1

CONTENTS

APPENDICES

CHAPTER 1
Business Plan

1.1 Introduction

Working musicians are often approached by friends, relatives, colleagues, or neighbors and asked, "Will you teach my son or daughter?" Perhaps you are already teaching; perhaps you have no intention of teaching privately; perhaps it's your primary goal to teach privately. Despite your projected plan, odds are that you will teach a private lesson at some point in your career.

> **Your independent music instruction experience should be as professional as possible.**

Regardless of whether independent private music instruction serves as an occasional occupation interspersed between performing jobs, supplemental income, or a sole financial source, it is necessary to consider this work as a business. Like any business, this venture should begin with a plan. You will be responsible for the education of others, spending your time, and using your talents; therefore, the process is deserving of a well-considered business plan.

How does one know what route to take if the final destination has yet to be determined? The final destination becomes clearer if a route is established. A business plan is needed to keep the business on track and in focus. Follow these steps to facilitate the path to a professional, independent music instruction experience:

1.2 Case Statement

Begin the business plan by formulating a case statement.

The case statement is a detailed directive for the business. It is usually 2-3 pages in length and includes the following:

1. The mission statement: Why does this business exist?
2. The goals: List the goals someone would expect to achieve through this association.
3. A brief history of the organization, personnel and professional information, and history.
4. The programs and services offered by the studio.
5. The financial workings of the studio, including tuition and attendance policies.
6. The facilities utilized and specific mechanics for the studio.
7. The plan for student and studio evaluation.

The **case statement** is built around the common questions of who, what, when, where, why, how, and how much. It is written in such a way that anyone unfamiliar with the organization or instructor could become aware of the studio's mission and purpose within the 10-15 minutes it would take to read. These components of the **case statement** should be published and distributed in new student packets which are made available to students and/or parents at the first lesson.

Also, the case statement serves as a guide for business planning. Each portion of the case statement will lay the foundation of the business plan and will guide the growth and implementation of the business.

1.2.1 Mission Statement

The first step of a case statement is a **mission statement.** A mission statement is the single summative objective for the business. This key message or phrase describes the business and defines the purpose of the organization. In the process of making decisions for the business, the mission statement will serve to direct the organization. It will describe in clear and concise language the fundamental values of this instructional situation. Even if you are working as an independent contractor, and regardless of whether you wish to teach five students or fifty students, any viable music instruction situation must have a mission statement.

1.2.2 Writing a Mission Statement

Writing a **mission statement** can be challenging. Review the following guidelines to aid in the writing of an original and all-encompassing mission statement.

Mission Statement Do's

Your studio's mission statement should
- inspire you to take action to start your business.
- require little or no explanation to the reader.
- be short on words, yet powerful in scope.
- be a clear and concise guide.
- consist of 6-20 easily remembered words that define the business.

Your studio's mission statement should reflect
- the passion you have for this endeavor.
- your personality.

> ### Mission Statement Don'ts
>
> *Your studio's mission statement should not*
> - be so complex that it can't be recited or remembered.
> - be so simple that it is trite.

Practical Application

Write three words that describe the studio you're planning to develop.

_____   _____   _____

Keeping in mind the information presented, use the 3 words you selected as the backbone of the mission statement for your studio.

_____

_____

_____

_____

Your business plan will begin to develop with the implementation of this mission statement.

1.3 Goals

The business plan will continue in its development with the implementation of goals. These goals will fall into two categories: personal and professional. However, one must keep in mind that the primary goal at all times is to make this experience as professional as possible.

Personal goals should
- be unpublished and remain personal.
- be established prior to professional goals.
- fall into 2 categories: educational and monetary.

1.3.1 Personal Educational Goals

In an attempt to minimize frustrations and stress, it is imperative that rational choices be made from the beginning of this endeavor. Making these choices will require that the educator look realistically at his or her ability level and personality. Excelling in musicianship and performing does not necessarily guarantee success as an educator. Establishing goals will aid in finding an instructional niche and help afford quality and success. Regardless of motivation, quality should still be the guide.

The aspiring independent music instructor has already selected the instrument of instruction, and musical expertise already exists. Therefore, in order for **personal educational goals** to be established, the initial consideration will be to determine the **age** and **ability** level of the students being sought. All teachers have a preconceived notion as to the age and/or the ability level they *want* to teach. However, is that desired level best suited to your personality and varied abilities?

Begin the process of determining the specific students the studio will seek by analyzing the private music instruction which you have received. Think about your most positive and negative experiences as a private student. There are many factors involved in these experiences including curriculum, lesson logistics, your age and state of mind, as well as teacher personality, skill level, and ability to instruct. By attempting to isolate specifics about your own experience, you will be able to better understand your own ability limitations and attributes. Contemplate and answer the following questions:

- What about the instruction you received worked well?
- Was the instruction lacking? If so, what specifically was it lacking?
- Were you taught theory, terminology, and general musicianship?
- What made your instruction excel?
- What made you seek another instructor?
- What makes an excellent instructor?

By answering these questions you will begin to find the direction that your educational goals should take. An effective, and ultimately a superior, private instruction experience begins by realizing the importance of the PIP formula which combines personality traits of the instructors, the instructor's ability to instruct their students, and the proficiency and knowledge level of the instructor.

> **PIP Formula for Effective Music Instruction**
> *Personality + Instruction + Proficiency*

1.3.2 Music Instruction Assessment

Assess what you believe makes the most effective, professional, and productive private musical experience for a student. Use the rating system below to evaluate each of the following aspects and/or traits that, in your opinion, make an effective instructor.

1 = poor
2 = fair
3 = average
4 = very good
5 = excellent

Rate the instructor's...

1. personal approachability

2. musical knowledge regarding technique

3. musical knowledge regarding theory

4. knowledge regarding curriculum and repertoire

5. musical experience

6. musical training

7. performing ability

8. ability to demonstrate

9. ability to impart knowledge and instruct

1.3.3 Personal Traits in Music Instruction Assessment

Look realistically and as objectively as possible and evaluate the same profile aspects and/or traits about yourself.

1 = poor
2 = fair
3 = average
4 = very good
5 = excellent

Rate your own...

1. personal approachability

2. musical knowledge regarding technique

3. musical knowledge regarding theory

4. knowledge regarding curriculum and repertoire

5. musical experience

6. musical training

7. performing ability

8. ability to demonstrate

9. ability to impart knowledge and instruct

Upon assessing your own traits of instruction, study the following table to help determine the level of student you are best suited to teach.

1.3.4 Music Instruction Assessment Results

Instructor Personality

Beginners	Asset	Score of 3-5 on question 1
Intermediate Students	Asset	Score of 3-5 on question 1
Advanced Students	Asset	Score of 3-5 on question 1

Instructor Musical Knowledge

Beginners	Asset	Score of 3-5 on questions 2 & 3
Intermediate Students	Necessity	Score of 5 on questions 2 & 3
Advanced Students	Necessity	Score of 5 on questions 2 & 3

Instructor Experience/Training

Beginners	Asset	Score of 3-5 on questions 5 & 6
Intermediate Students	Asset	Score of 3-5 on questions 5 & 6
Advanced Students	Necessity	Score of 5 on questions 5 & 6

Performing/Ability to Demonstrate

Beginners	Asset	Responses of 3-5 on questions 7 & 8
Intermediate Students	Asset	Responses of 3-5 on questions 7 & 8
Advanced Students	Necessity	Response of 5 on questions 7 & 8

Instructor Knowledge of Curriculum/Literature

Beginners	Necessity	Response of 5 on question 4*
Intermediate Students	Asset	Responses of 3-5 on question 4†
Advanced Students	Necessity	Response of 5 on question 4†

* in regard to curriculum
† in regard to literature

Instructor Ability to Impart Knowledge

Beginners	Necessity	Response of 5 on question 9
Intermediate Students	Necessity	Response of 5 on question 9
Advanced Students	Necessity	Response of 5 on question 9

Now determine which level student you believe that you are best equipped to teach.

Musicians who are performing and teaching today are in these positions due to the influence of their previous effective instructors. It is your goal to be an instructor with a similar degree of lasting influence. Where will you find your most productive niche? If your scores are on the lower end of the scales, perhaps you are not ready to join the market at this time.

Look objectively at the results from the PIP formula questions. You should now begin to write your personal educational goals compensating for the weaknesses and capitalizing on the strengths that were pinpointed in the profile questions.

The Private Music Instruction Manual: A Guide for the Independent Music Educator • Rebecca Osborn

Realize that the goals, which seek specific ages or ability levels, will greatly increase personal instructional success and will enable both you and the student to achieve the highest level of satisfaction. Decide whether to pursue any or all of these groups of students:

- preschool and early elementary beginners [strings/piano]
- traditional-age beginners (Grades 2-5) [all instruments]
- adult beginners
- intermediate students of all ages
- advanced students of all ages

Once you begin to discover the ages and ability levels of the students that are best suited to your abilities, review the following generalizations about students.

1.3.5 Generalizations Regarding Beginners

- Young beginners require much patience and energy.
- Adolescent beginners require much motivation.
- Adult beginners require much encouragement.

Young and adolescent beginners often do not require as much instructional explanation. For example, if you are explaining a theory concept, a young or adolescent beginner generally doesn't care about specifics. These students spend their entire day taking part in an educational process in which knowledge is presented and they are taught to accept it as such. They generally accept the things their instructor tells them as fact and without question.

Adult beginners, on the other hand, need and require additional explanation. Adults are accustomed to being in charge as they manage their homes, lives, and businesses. You are introducing something totally foreign to a competent and intelligent adult who will require much clarification. Contrary to school-age students, adults have become accustomed to understanding; children spend a significant percentage of their day not questioning and simply accepting knowledge.

1.3.6 Generalizations Regarding Adult Beginners

Adult students are making a major commitment with their instruction decision. They know and understand the financial obligations and generally approach their lessons quite seriously. Often an adult does not have a successful experience because they have not allotted the time necessary to reach the desired proficiency. It would be advantageous to advise them of the time commitment necessary before lessons commence.

There is frequently a "catch 22" situation with adults; they are extreme perfectionists, but because of time limitations are unable to perform at the levels they desire. A high dropout rate occurs among beginning adult students.

1.3.7 Generalizations Regarding Intermediate Level Students

Regardless of the age of this student, musical technique and literature aspects are stronger than during the beginning informational aspects of instruction. Intermediate students enjoy varied literature styles and genres as they have now sufficiently advanced to be able to master and appreciate them. These students have gained enough knowledge to have respect for performing and will respond well to instruction that includes demonstration.

1.3.8 Generalizations Regarding Advanced Students

These students benefit greatly from the musical knowledge and expertise that an excellent instructor can impart. Advanced level students should possess near mastery of theory and technique; however, frequent cases exist in which these elements do not coincide with the level of performance that the student has achieved.

Case #1

You have decided to teach intermediate and advanced level private students. However, six months into the business, great frustration has developed in teaching an intermediate level student who has transferred from another instructor with a bevy of problems. Scales, technique, and theory have never been stressed, yet the student can "get through" a piece of challenging literature. Reteaching must occur in many areas.

Possible Solution #1
Be prepared to broaden your personal goals if necessary. Offer private lessons to beginners as well as intermediate and advanced students. Realize that the frustration experienced by teaching beginning students will perhaps be less than the frustration that would come from correcting technique problems that have festered for an extended period of time in the intermediate and advanced students.

Possible Solution #2
Widen the demographic area involved in the hopes of attracting more advanced students while dropping the intermediate students.

Warning
Be prepared to lose this student. It is possible that they will think that they are being held back because you are spending too much time on the basics.

Would you use either of these solutions or one of your own? Why?

Case #2

You know yourself to be very patient, have a strong personality, and wish to teach only beginners; however, six months into the business, it's not as fun you thought it would be. The love for children and instruction exists, but you are bored by repeatedly explaining the same basic concepts time and time again.

Possible Solution #1
Allow yourself to take a few intermediate students. If you have a studio with twenty students who all began instruction at or about the same time, you are spending much of your instructional time covering the same material, listening to the same pieces, and even hearing the same mistakes. Allow yourself the luxury of teaching someone who can play musically. You owe it to yourself.

Would you use this solution or one of your own? Why?

1.4 Monetary Personal Goal

Personal finances will determine what financial goals need to be established. Is this endeavor a primary or supplemental source of income? The answer to this question will resolve many personal goal issues.

Case #3

Your cash flow has not grown at the anticipated or expected level because the number of students is not as great as you desired.

Possible Solution #1
Be prepared to reasonably broaden the personal goals. Perhaps their specificity is limiting your financial success.

Possible Solution #2
There could be many reasons for cash flow problems, but most obvious is lack of students. Location of the studio, advertising, scheduling, and lesson prices are several possible reasons for monetary problems. Look specifically at each of these issues to determine what may be causing or contributing to your problem.

Would you use this solution or one of your own? Why?

Go for the Goals!

After considering both monetary and educational aspects of personal goals, put them in writing. Read them, review them, revise them, and then live by them. What goal is more important to you: educational, monetary, or a combination of the two? Make your compromises now, not once you get started, and remember...

> *Your independent music instruction experience should be as professional as possible.*

1.5 Professional Goals

This business and your teaching are responsible for the music education and development of students. It is for this reason that professional goals should be written with educationally-objective influences. These goals should be published so that they are available upon request by prospective or current students. The goals should be in the form of typical lesson plans and can be as detailed or general as desired.

Details of professional goals should be determined by
• the ability level of the students.
• the specific curriculum utilized.

Goal format for all level students should include:

Materials
List curriculum or text used.

Objectives
The student will be able to
• list theory concepts you believe are necessary.
• list technique concepts you believe are necessary.
• list performance concepts you believe are necessary.

Evaluation
Provide progress reports
Provide graded lessons
Host performances
Specify sequence of curriculum
(*i.e.* how students will move from one level instruction book to the next)

1.6 Summary

Begin any independent music instruction with a business plan by formulating a case statement that will serve as a foundational guide.

Step one of a case statement is a mission statement, *i.e.* defining a description of the business and its objectives which will serve to direct the organization. The mission statement should be clear, concise, and easily understood by the reader.

Determining goals for your business plan fall into two categories: personal and professional. Personal (unpublished) goals which are educational and monetary, should be established first. Educational goals will aid in deciding your instructional niche. Take into consideration the type of student the studio will be seeking by analyzing the positive and negative aspects of your own experience. To assist in this process, use the PIP formula, compensating for weaknesses and capitalizing on strengths.

Goals which seek specific age/ability levels will greatly increase instructional success and help you deem which ages and abilities will enable both you and the student to achieve the highest level of satisfaction.

Monetary personal goals can be determined by considering if this is a supplemental or primary source of income. Personal educational and monetary goals should be put in writing. Read, review, revise, and live by them.

At the outset, be aware of the generalizations which characterize each age group and each ability level and learn to adjust according to their individual needs.

Professionalism is a must. Professional goals should be determined by the category of the student and by considering the specific curriculum used to achieve objectives with an ongoing evaluation process.

Practical Application

Begin the writing of a case statement for your independent music instruction business.

1. Finalize the mission statement.
2. Write educational, monetary, and professional goals in a clear and concise manner.

CHAPTER 2
Curriculum

2.1 Program Offerings

2.1.1 Choosing a Text, Method, or Series

Deciding upon the instructional curriculum to be used in private teaching can be very challenging. New materials are published constantly. Remain aware and informed of the latest choices and current trends. Do not allow the selection to be made solely on the basis of personal comfort level. Also, do not simply choose the same methods which you used as a student just because you are familiar with them. There are many curricular selections available which appeal to various learning styles. Take time to study and evaluate these different options. Choices should offer the well-rounded education that all students deserve.

Piano curricula continue to be in the forefront of text offerings; the choices in piano are plentiful, and the many options are educationally sound. In comparison, there are fewer instrumental choices. Voice curricula are practically nonexistent.

There are many texts and methods available. Below is a list of possibilities for your perusal.

Vocal Methods

Adventures in Singing by Clifton Ware
Basics of Singing by Jan Schmidt
The Estelle Liebling Vocal Course by Estelle Liebling
Sight Singing Made Simple by David Bauguess
Sight Singing: The Complete Method for Singers by Mike Campbell
Singing Technique by Carl Hogset
Structure of Singing: System and Art in Vocal Technique by Richard Miller
The Voice: A Spiritual Approach to Singing, Speaking, and Communicating by
    Miriam Arman
Teaching Kids to Sing by Kenneth Phillips

Instrumental Methods

Accent on Achievement by John O'Reilly
Alfred's Basic Band Methods by Sandy Feldstein and John O'Reilly
All for Strings by Anderson and Frast
Band Plus by Jim Swearingen and Barbara Buehlman
Band Today by Perez
Belwin Band Builder by Warner Bros. Publishing
Belwin Elementary Band Method by Warner Bros. Publishing
Belwin String Builder by Warner Bros. Publishing
Best in Class Band Method by Forque and Anderson
Essential Elements by Hal Leonard Publishing
First Division Band Method by Proctor
Now Go Home and Practice by Heritage Music Press
Rubank Elementary, Intermediate, and Advanced Methods by Rubank
Standard of Excellence by Bruce Pearson
Strictly Strings by Dillon and O'Reilly
Suzuki Method by Suzuki
Yamaha Band Student by Feldstein and O'Reilly

Piano Methods

Basic Piano & adult by Michael Aaron
Alfred's Basic Piano, adult & supplementary by Alfred Publishing
Basic Piano, adult & supplementary by Bastien
Basic Piano & adult by Bradley
John Brimhall Piano Method by John Brimhall
Step by Step & *A Dozen a Day* by Edna Mae Burnam
Piano Course by Alfred D'Auberge
Basic Piano, adult & supplementary by Eckstein
Basic Piano & supplementary by Faber and Faber
Basic Piano & adult by Leila Fletcher
Basic Piano & jazz by William Gillock
Basic Piano, adult & supplementary by David Carr Glover
Basic Piano & supplementary by David Hirschberg
Student Piano Library by Hal Leonard Publishing
Music Pathways: Piano Discoveries by Olson, Bianchi, and Blickenstaff
Basic Piano & supplementary by Mark Nevin
Basic Piano, Adult, & supplementary by Walter and Carol Noona
Robert Pace Piano Series by Robert Pace
Chords and Scales by Ada Richter
Basic Piano, adult & supplementary by John W. Schaum
Basic Piano, adult & supplementary by John Thompson

For further assistance in selecting a piano series, consider consulting the Bastien textbook, *How to Teach Piano Successfully* ISBN 0-8497-6168-9. This helpful guide may also serve to help establish a piano curriculum. Also consider *The Well Tempered Keyboard Instructor* by Gordon Uszler and McBride Smith.

2.1.2 Supplementing a Text, Method, or Series

In the event that a series has been chosen that seems lax in theory studies, consider using one of the following for supplemental theory instruction:

Theory Supplements

Essentials of Music Theory by Alfred Publishing
Fundamentals of Piano Theory by Keith Snell & Martha Ashleigh
Jazz Theory Book by Mark Levine
Master Theory by Peters and Yoder
Practical Theory by Sandy Feldstein
Theory and Harmony for Everyone by Dean Bye
Theory and Harmony for the Contemporary Musician by Arnie Berle

---

2.1.3 Curriculum Offerings Checklist

Use the following checklist as a curriculum evaluation. Analyze your prospective curriculum and circle your rating.

N/A   not applicable
1   not at all
2   slightly
3   somewhat
4   definitely
5   excellent

There is a logical progression of material presented.
N/A 1 2 3 4 5   *Specific Comments:*_____

There is a good blending of information incorporating technique, history, and theory, in conjunction with the repertoire.
N/A 1 2 3 4 5   *Specific Comments:*_____

The series offers beginning, intermediate, and/or advanced levels of study.
N/A 1 2 3 4 5   *Specific Comments:*_____

The beginning level is visually appealing.
N/A 1 2 3 4 5   *Specific Comments:*_____

The intermediate and advanced levels offer visuals which lend themselves to easy legibility incorporating appropriate printed note size, measure placement, and page turns.
N/A 1 2 3 4 5   *Specific Comments:*_____

The beginning and intermediate levels include chapter summaries and/or questioning sections.
N/A 1 2 3 4 5   *Specific Comments:*_____

The repertoire selected for instruction offers a strong mix of styles and/or composers.
N/A 1 2 3 4 5   *Specific Comments:*_____

The series is suited for adolescent and/or adult students.
N/A 1 2 3 4 5   *Specific Comments:*_____

The series is suited for younger students.
N/A 1 2 3 4 5   *Specific Comments:*_____

The series demonstrates appropriate scope and sequence by moving smoothly from one instructional level to the next.
N/A 1 2 3 4 5   *Specific Comments:*_____

The series offers and encourages opportunities for creativity through the use of improvisation and composition.
N/A 1 2 3 4 5   *Specific Comments:*_____

This series offers a well-rounded music education.
N/A 1 2 3 4 5   *Specific Comments:*_____

Supplemental materials are required when using this series because the content lacks important lessons.
      Yes   No   *Specific Comments:*_____

Supplemental materials would not be required (but still may be used) because the series is sufficiently complete in scope.
      Yes   No   *Specific Comments:*_____

Consult the curriculum offerings assessment when selecting an instructional curriculum. Using the curriculum assessment as a guide, obtain reading copies of sample methods to determine whether or not you would use this instructional method for:

- Beginning Students
  List your reasons why or why not.
- Intermediate Students
  List your reasons why or why not.
- Adult Students
  List your reasons why or why not.

2.2 Technology in Teaching

Contemplate the use of technology in your studio. Computers make an outstanding teaching tool for both the educator and the student.

There is quality software available for music instruction. These software titles can produce original worksheets and offer concentrated instruction where needed. They allow the possibility to tailor-make instruction for specific needs without much instructor effort or time commitment. There is also theory software which takes no teacher preparation and offers a logical and thorough study.

Many students will respond to computer instruction much more readily than to a traditional paper and pencil approach. Today's students are acclimated to using computers in their learning. They also spend hours playing games and now, thanks to the available software, can play games to learn music. Music computer games bait the student into learning and raise their level of proficiency through point totals, competition, and high scores. The games are presented in a visually and aurally appealing format. Consider some of the following titles:

> ### *Educational Music Software*
>
> *Music Ace I & II*
> *Music Maid*
> *Music Lessons*
> *Musicus*
> *Adventures in Musicland*
> *The Musical World of Professor Piccolo*
> *Discovering Music*
> *Melody Music Lab*
> *Practica Musica*

In seeking music publishing applications with MIDI (Musical Instrument Digital Interface) compatibility, consider:

> ### *Notation and Sequencing Music Software*
>
> *Print Music* by Coda
> *Amadeus Opus* by Sincrosoft
> *Cakewalk Home Studio* by Cakewalk
> *Freestyle* by Mark of The Unicorn
> *Metro* by Cakewalk
> *Sibelius* by Coda
> *Finale* by Coda
> *Encore* by Passport

The following checklist is helpful when evaluating software.

2.2.1 Software Evaluation Checklist

Use the following checklist as a software evaluation. Analyze your prospective software application and circle your rating.

> N/A   not applicable
> 1   not at all
> 2   slightly
> 3   somewhat
> 4   definitely
> 5   excellent
>
> Is easy to use and user friendly .... N/A 1 2 3 4 5
>
> Has instructional value .... N/A 1 2 3 4 5
>
> Addresses concepts of music notation and music intonation ... N/A 1 2 3 4 5
>
> Is appropriately entertaining .... N/A 1 2 3 4 5
>
> Is age appropriate .... N/A 1 2 3 4 5
>
> Is visually appealing .... N/A 1 2 3 4 5
>
> Is aurally appealing .... N/A 1 2 3 4 5
>
> Demonstrates strong subject accuracy .... N/A 1 2 3 4 5

2.3 Basic Private Lesson Format

Regardless of length, private lessons should generally have similar format. Instructional concepts won't change, only time allotments will.

It is essential to know the objective with each student and have an individualized instructional plan. These objectives may evolve and change as the rapport between the student and instructor develops.

Materials Needed
Have any text, supplemental materials, CDs, cassettes, tape players, *etc.* in place and prepared before the lesson.

Introduction
Chat as instrumentalists get out instruments and vocalists get set up. Ask about health, amount of time given to practice during the week, any performances that took place since the last meeting, *etc.* Such conversation will serve to help you know and understand the student.

Teaching Technique
Begin with scales and warm-ups. Use this time to work on hand position, alternate fingerings, embouchure, bowing, tongue position, breathing, vocal placement, *etc.*

Teaching Sight-Reading
Sight reading allows an instant opportunity to include theory in the lesson. Musical notation including keys, time signatures, rhythm, musical symbols, and editors' marks can and should be defined, discussed, and analyzed at this time.

Teaching Literature
Work on the literature assigned. Allow the student to perform the prepared piece once. On longer works, allow the student to perform the entire section assigned. Listening to a longer section affords you an overview of ongoing problems, but more importantly allows the student to have a sense of completion and success. After one run-through, go back and take apart the literature, giving attention to the specifics.

In addition to note accuracy, techniques, and artistry, students should be taught to thoroughly analyze the selection being studied. Insist upon written information in this analysis so that pupils will eventually learn to formulate this kind of information independently. Analysis options should include:

- the work's title and its significance
- pertinent information about the composer and compositional style
- historical period, dates, and related information
- textual source (for vocal music), poet, stylistic period, translation, meaning
- formal structure: binary, ternary, rondo, through-composed, or other
- harmonic treatment, basic tonality, or modality
- melodic treatment: contours of the melodic line
- movement or skips of pitch levels, melodic patterns, or use of notation
- significant rhythmic treatments or figures
- significant dynamic treatments

Complete this part of the lesson by assigning any new materials.

Closure
Finish by performing the piece studied during the lesson, reinforcing points made during the course of the lesson, and tying together concepts of the lesson. Be sure to praise the student for any progress and challenge them to continue developing as a musician.

Review practice requirements for the coming week.

2.4 Practice Requirements

To achieve a successful performance level, the student must know and understand the instructor's practice goals for them. **Beginning** and **Intermediate** students who are not adults need specific instructions regarding practice requirements and procedures. It is the responsibility of the instructor to help the student structure their practice time. There should be no question in the minds of either the student or parents as to what is required and expected.

Often an **Advanced** student may need some guidance regarding the specifics of practice needs. For example, if the same problem or mistake keeps occurring, it can probably be traced to faulty practice. Remind the student that each time they repeat the mistake, they have flawed their practice, which in turn will reinforce the error in performance. In order to improve, a student needs a clear goal. Ask for specifics about their practice of a particular problem passage:

- Have they worked at developing the correct kinesthetic reflex necessary for a secure performance?
- Have they isolated a particular passage too much and now it has lost its flow and ability to integrate into the whole?

2.4.1 Practice Information for All Students

1. Efficient Practice Habits. The more efficient their practice habits, the more confident their performance of the piece will be.
2. Procedures for Memorization. Include procedures for memorization in your practice requirements.
3. Time Investment Required. Students require an indication of the time investment expected of them. Never assume anything when teaching. Be as specific as possible when mapping out your expectations of any student.

Study the practice log (Appendix A) and parent guides (Appendices M, N, and O) found the Appendices section. Please note how specific these instructions are. These guides can serve as a prototype for the information you will use in your own studio. Remember that beginners and many parents of beginners will need to understand what is needed for successful practice. These guidelines should be presented to students at the beginning of their private instruction experience.

2.4.2 Practice Logs

Design a practice log or require students to purchase an assignment book. Insist that students keep a notebook that is solely for lesson assignments and notes. Assignments must be written, especially for younger students (through grade 6).

There are two ways to designate practice assignments to students:
1. Amount of time required
2. Number of performing repetitions required

Be astute enough to see the needs of a specific student. Determine which style of practice will best suit the individual student personality and ultimately produce the best results.

Number of playing repetitions required
> for example: "Hickory Dickory Dock" 5x daily
> *Pros*
> * Gives a definite message to the student.
> * Supplies added reinforcement for success as the student marks off each time they play.
> * Allows for continuous practice through repetitions.
> *Cons*
> * Encourages a student to "play through" music rather than practice music; they are so interested in the end product that the process suffers.
> * Musicianship may suffer.

Amount of practice time required
> for example: 25 minutes daily M-F
> *Pros*
> * Allows a parent to keep track of time.
> * Encourages a time-oriented, motivated student.
> *Cons*
> * Allows an unmotivated student to not utilize their practice time effectively.
> * Emphasizes time rather than performance quality.

2.4.3 Parent Signatures

Some teachers require that a parent sign the practice log or assignment book. This signature serves as a guideline for parents to monitor practice and as a motivational tool for some students. Regardless of the signature, the insightful instructor will know instantly if and what kind of practice occurred since the last lesson simply by the performance of the student.

2.4.4 Organizational Materials

Require students to have a folder and/or bag. Students of all ages and levels need a specific location to store their materials.

Practical Application

Refer to the sample practice log in Appendix A and then design a practice log which you feel will best meet the needs of your students. Consider the following in its design:

- Spaces for student name, date, and other information
- Space for instructor to write in assignment for week
- Time divisions (days, minutes, other increments)
- Section for student to record their materials practiced
- Space for parent signature
- Other features

2.5 Curriculum Supplements

2.5.1 Personal Library

Upon selection of curriculum, it is possible that you will still need or want to occasionally supplement repertoire with materials from your personal library.

Any and all personal supplements that are used such as sheet music, musical collections, and texts should be monitored by your own checkout system. Musicians are notorious for "borrowing" music and not returning it. Many of us have music in our own library that has someone else's name inside the front cover. Use a similar system if you decide to loan equipment such as metronomes, microphones, CDs, videos, or audio cassettes.

Make sure that a written record is kept of any loaned materials.

Student Name	Item Borrowed	Date

2.5.2 Computer Instruction

In conjunction with or in place of a weekly lesson, offer a student one-on-one time in computer music instruction. Use computer applications to encourage composition and strengthen theory knowledge.

2.5.3 Group Instruction

All students can benefit from experiences in group instruction in addition to and/or in conjunction with private instruction.

- Substitute the fifth lesson in a five-lesson month with a group or class experience.
- Substitute one monthly private lesson with a group experience. Offer the group lesson once per month on the same day as the usual private lesson. For example, the first 5 students who normally have a Tuesday lesson will meet for a group lesson at 5:00 on the second Tuesday of each month.
- Add group lessons in addition to the student's regularly scheduled lesson time.
- Add a summer class as an added incentive to keep students interested in summer lessons.
- Add regular or occasional Saturday morning classes during the school year.

The location and facility availability for group lessons may be a problem or challenge. Search for an alternate teaching location or plan to adjust to cramped quarters and space limitations.

Group/Class instruction can yield several positive results:

- Afford students the opportunity to improve performing skills in a constructive environment with their peers.
- Help students become more astute listeners.
- Elevate critiquing abilities of each student through observation and discussions of performance.
- Provide a forum for presentation of information through games and activities that can only be achieved through group participation.

A performance class is another group instruction option which could afford many opportunities:

- Encourage or require students to perform for and critique each another.
- Offer a master class with a guest instructor.
- Ask a friend or colleague to present an evening of group instruction, critiquing, or performing for the class.
- Offer a monthly class in theory or history.

Explore teaching non-performing concepts in a classroom setting. Group instruction lends itself to games, friendly rivalry, and group activities, while it serves to solidify concepts that have been presented during private instruction. These group experiences add variety to teaching. It would be advisable to organize these small classes with homogeneous age and ability levels to afford maximum enjoyment and ease of instruction.

Group/Class instruction should include the following activities:
- Student performances for peers.
- Invite a guest instructor who would reinforce concepts already learned.
- Applied music instruction using ensemble exercises and scales with critiques and performances.
- Music theory utilizing games and activities stressing music elements with brief lectures on the same.
- History and appreciation including listening, discussions, and short lectures.

Group/Class instruction in applied music should include:
- ensemble exercises and scales.
- ensemble *and* individual performances.
- ensemble *and* individual critiques.

Group/Class instruction in theory should include:
- games reinforcing the elements of music.
- activities stressing the elements of music.
- informal lectures on music.
- improvisational activities.
- aural exercises.

Group/Class instruction in history/appreciation should include:
- listening.
- informational lectures.
- discussions.

Group instruction lends itself to friendly competition as it serves to solidify concepts that have been presented during private instruction. These experiences add variety to teaching and give both the student and the instructor a change of pace.

This addition to the curriculum is well worth the extra effort as it will produce noticeable, positive results in the vast majority of students.

The Private Music Instruction Manual: A Guide for the Independent Music Educator • Rebecca Osborn

2.6 Summary

Accept the challenge of choosing a text, method, or series by being informed about the latest materials available. Make choices based not on your comfort level, but after careful study, on which series offers a well-rounded education. Piano curricula are plentiful, but there are fewer choices for other instruments and less still for voice instruction. Analyze the series being contemplated and rate it considering student appeal in relation to age/ability level and desired goals.

The computer is an invaluable teaching tool, and students respond readily to its use. Become knowledgeable about current software available, and evaluate carefully. To make sure the pupil is effectively using the computer, consider offering a one-on-one session in lieu of or in addition to the weekly lesson.

Use an instructional format for lessons with individual objectives for each student. All materials needed should be readily available. Every lesson should include technique, sight reading, and a variety of literature with analysis to enhance the performance of the music.

Students should complete the lesson with a clear understanding of what should be practiced. It is important to provide instruction addressing the ways to effectively use practice time with specific guidance for both practice and memorization. Involve the parents of school-age students by requiring a signature verifying practice time. These students should have a folder or bag in which to store their lesson materials.

Be sure to keep a written record of any materials loaned. Establish checkout procedures and discuss liability for lost or damaged materials.

Group/class instruction is valuable, and there are a variety of ways they can be incorporated into the schedule. Organize these classes homogeneously, and include, performance, applied music, theory, history, and appreciation. The results of this type of instruction will be rewarding · allowing for the development of well-rounded, knowledgeable musicians, who are actively increasing their artistic level.

Practical Application

Using the basic private lesson format in this chapter, devise a plan for an intermediate level student. Include:
- your method course of choice.
- practice requirements.

Plan a group lesson to teach and reinforce the concept of rhythm. This class for students in grades 2-6 should last 45 minutes. Include the following:
- lecture and explanation.
- listening.
- written work including a worksheet.
- games and/or activities.

CHAPTER 3
Lesson Dynamics

3.1 Lesson Dynamics

Once a business plan has been established and curricular concerns have been contemplated, the more specific, day-to-day lesson dynamics can be addressed. Three areas which require consideration include scheduling, lesson tuition, and lesson cancellation policies.

3.1.1 Establish Definite Hours

Every store and commercial business has posted business hours; your business should be no different. Establish hours of operation from the onset of the business and reconfirm them frequently. This action perpetuates the notion that you are a professional and should be treated as such. Regarding in-home studios, unfortunately, there may be some students who will request a different lesson time simply because they know the business is in the home. When no times are established, students may feel that your time is not valuable and may make unreasonable requests. By adhering to posted hours, lesson times will be kept within the parameters which have been set for the business.

How much time will you devote to your teaching each week?

Establish a teaching schedule and do not deviate from it. If you are prone to cancellations and missed lessons, then your students will be prone to cancellations and missed lessons. Do not be tempted to call and move someone's lesson time simply because you have a void there from another student cancellation. This demonstrates that you are too flexible and the student will expect the same courtesy of a switched lesson time when they have a conflict. This could also serve to encourage a bold or brash student or parent to make demands on your time.

3.1.2 Duration of Lessons

30 minutes
 Pros
 - These lessons will move quickly. Neither you nor the student will likely become bored!
 - These lessons may allow you to make money in a shorter amount of time.

 Cons
 - There will not always be weekly opportunities to include theory and sight-reading.
 - These lessons are challenging to keep on time. If you have to do any discussion with parents (i.e. lesson changes or conflicts, student progress, or any other business including personal health breaks) you will ultimately cheat the lesson time in order to stay on schedule. Realistically, this lesson will last 23-25 minutes.

40 minutes; scheduled on the :45's
 Pros
 - These lessons are easier to keep on schedule.
 - These lessons allow more opportunity to include theory, and/or sight-reading at each meeting.

 Cons
 - These lessons can produce awkward scheduling.

55 minutes; scheduled on the hour
 Pros
 - These lessons are excellent for more advanced students; history, theory, technique, and style can be included.

 Cons
 - These lessons are very difficult to fill for beginning students. That hour may seem like an eternity!

3.1.3 Day or Days of Instruction

In sparsely populated areas it will become necessary for you to study local events and/or calendars. You and the local ballet teacher or art instructor will likely be competing for the same students. If, for example, there is only one night for ballet at the dance studio, think about opting for another evening to offer your instruction. In a heavily populated area there need not be much concern regarding time conflicts with other programs and offerings.

3.1.4 Other Scheduling Considerations

Investigate the length of the instructional day in the area school districts where your service will be offered. This will aid in determining the time of day that school-age students will be available and may help to guide studio lesson scheduling.

1. Save after-school times in the schedule for younger students. These students have minimal extracurricular involvements which allow for fewer scheduling conflicts.
2. Week nights lend themselves to better attendance than weekends.
3. If it is feasible to student and teacher, consider offering a lesson time that is before the beginning of the school day.
4. Offer times during the day for adults and home schooled students.
5. There will always be some conflicts regardless of the day and/or time.

If the teaching schedule includes an entire evening—early afternoon through the evening hours—decide if you will take a break for dinner, refueling, and general mental health. Are you the type that will need this rejuvenation, or do you prefer to teach straight through and have your break and rest at the end of the evening? Decide which schedule suits your personality and set up your instructional time accordingly.

If there is not a specific waiting area for the studio, insist that students be dropped off and picked up no more than ten minutes before or after their assigned lesson time. Your service is music instruction, not child care.

It is best to start a new schedule in the fall. Although spring is generally considered the season for new beginnings, this is not true in any kind of education program. Use the spring calendar to determine and publicize hours of instruction for the upcoming fall. Begin a new schedule the week after most schools return in the fall session. People are ready to get back to work in the fall, and for many studios, the number of students enrolled will be the greatest at this time.

It is often difficult to maintain your schedule in the late spring and summer months. After spring break, interest often wanes and cancellations become plentiful. Encourage students to continue lessons through the summer months by offering incentives and differing methods of instruction. Consider bringing in guest clinicians, taking a field trip, having a party, or planning performances for local nursing homes as possible additions to the summer curriculum. See Chapter 7 for detailed listings of summer and holiday incentives.

Try to minimize distractions in the in-home studio. Put an answering machine on the phone, hire a babysitter for your child, start dinner preparations when students are not present, prepare food that does not require attention. Take breaks on your own time, not on a student's. Do not slight or cheat a student of scheduled lesson time.

3.2 Establish Lesson *Tuition*

Tuition is paid for everything from preschool to a college education. Lesson charges should be referred to as "tuition." This term "tuition" exemplifies the seriousness of the professional education the studio is offering. The public treats "tuition" more seriously than "fees" or "charges."

3.2.1 Establish Pricing

There are five factors involved in determining the lesson charge.

1. Instructor credentials
2. Studio location
3. Studio expenses
4. Length of the lesson
5. Type of lesson provided

Charge tuition that is in keeping with a professional service.

3.2.2 Instructor Credentials

You have paid for your own training with both money and time; your students are expecting to pay you for these investments. Your experience is also valuable. Specific expertise is what sets you apart from all others. Consider any unique offerings you may have, *i.e.* banjo, blues guitar, or bag pipes. Factor in all of these credential considerations when establishing tuition.

3.2.3 Studio Location

Establish rates that are competitive in the geographic area surrounding the studio. Call music stores, churches, schools and universities, and inquire about local music instructional rates. These rates are generally determined by the cost of living and the socioeconomic makeup of the community that will be serviced. Studio location may well be the greatest determining factor in establishing lesson tuition.

3.2.4 Studio Expenses

Your expenses will fall into three categories:

Setup	*Annual*	*On-going*
equipment	professional dues	newsletters/mailings
materials	recitals	insurance
library		rent/mortgage
		utilities
		consumables/incentives
		facility maintenance
		instrument maintenance
		advertising

Annual and on-going expenses are obvious business expenditures which can and should be recouped by their inclusion in the tuition.

It will be difficult to estimate what the on-going and recital costs will be before the fact; however, it is VERY important to do this research exactly.

3.2.5 Lesson Length and Type

The longer the lesson, the greater the charge should be.

Will lessons be private or group lessons? Private lessons should obviously cost more than group lessons.

Initiate tuition rates only after studying and researching all five price-determining factors.

3.2.6 General Tuition Considerations

Do not underprice tuition. If prices are too low, astute clients will tend to question the quality of the product that they are about to receive. The student who is seeking quality instruction and longevity in the student/teacher relationship is willing to pay the price for substance.

If someone calls and the first question they ask is, "How much do you charge?" odds are they are not seeking the first-rate instruction you offer. They may even offer that they can get lessons elsewhere for a greatly reduced price. An appropriate response might be to assure them that your instruction is top quality, and that generally, one gets what one pays for in music instruction. Do not be discouraged by these calls, as those students seldom stay in the program longer than a month or two. The dropout rate among students who choose substandard instruction is tremendous. In my experience, the drop-out rate in private lessons has been around 90%. So, do not feel badly when you hear a monetary response. Save your time and knowledge for someone who is appreciative of it. Remind yourself that in life, you get what you pay for.

In addition to tuition for lessons many studios charge additional fees including:
- Materials fees to cover studio overhead and supplies.
- Recital fees to cover recital expenditures.
- Book fees collected for methods, materials, and sheet music.

Important Notes...

- **It is easier to lower your prices than to raise them.**
- **The more you are in demand, the more you can demand.**

3.2.7 Payment Policy Overview

After determining a pricing policy, establish a payment policy. Establish how tuition will be collected.

Payment Policy Options

Individual Lessons
Students pay for each lesson received.

Monthly
Students pay a flat monthly rate regardless of number of lessons received. Considering that there are four lessons in most months, but that there are some months with holidays and some five lesson months.

Semester or Term
Students pay a flat semester rate. Be aware of the total number of lessons which will be offered during the time frame.

3.2.8 Payment Policy Specifics

There are several options when selecting a payment policy. Examine the options presented here and chose which, if any, will work for your particular instructional situation.

1. **Individual Lessons**
   Students pay for each lesson received.
   Pros
   - Cash flow is constant.
   - No need to "chase" money for lessons attended.

   Cons
   - It takes instructional time from each lesson to collect money and write receipts.
   - Unless studio policy firmly and specifically states, there may be difficulty retrieving money for missed or cancelled lessons.

2. **Monthly**
   Students pay a flat monthly rate. Lesson tuition is due at the first lesson of each month.
   Pros
   - You will never need to retrieve money for lessons taught because you do not teach the lesson without payment.
   - You will have fewer interruptions in instructional time.
   - This assures you a monthly income.
   - There will be consolidated bookkeeping.

   Cons
   - There will be complaints if a student pays for a lesson that must be cancelled and is not reimbursed.

3. **Variation: Monthly; pay by the 15th of the month**
   Pros
   - This allows families with financial challenges the chance for a more liberal payment policy.
   - This assures you a monthly income.

   Cons
   - Will need to establish a late fee program for those who do not pay by the 15th.
   - Bookkeeping is increased.
   - Possible for a student to take one lesson, never return, and never pay for the one lesson received.
   - There will be complaints if a student pays for a lesson that must be cancelled and is not reimbursed.

4. **Semester or Term**
   Students pay a flat semester rate at the beginning of the term.
   Pros
   - This provides the greatest amount of financial security.
   - Bookkeeping is minimal.

   Cons
   - Possible short-term students are deterred.
   - Students/parents who are not prepared for 100% commitment may be deterred.
   - There will be complaints if a student pays for a lesson that must be cancelled and is not reimbursed.

5. **Variation: Semester or Term; pay by semester or term in two increments.**
   One payment at the first lesson; second payment partway through the semester.
   Pros
   - A fair amount of financial security is provided.
   - A fair amount of bookkeeping is necessary.
   - Allows families with financial challenges the chance for a more liberal payment policy.

   Cons
   - Opportunity for mid-semester dropout is allowed.
   - Will need to establish a late-fee program for those who do not pay second payment on time.
   - There will be complaints if a student pays for a lesson that must be cancelled and is not reimbursed.

In general, select the policy which you feel is the most fair, professional, and logical and which gives the student the least opportunity to treat instruction lightly.

3.3 Cancellation Policy

Cancellations are inevitable and need to be addressed. **Specify the studio policy and adhere to it.**

3.3.1 Cancellation Policy Considerations

- Will the studio offer refunds or credits for student-generated cancellations?
- Will the studio offer refunds or credits for teacher-generated cancellations?
- Will the studio have excused and unexcused student absences?
- Will the studio offer make-up lessons for teacher-generated cancellations?
- Will the studio offer makeup lessons for student-generated cancellations?
- Will the studio have closings on days that the local school district has closings?
- Will the studio have weather-related cancellations?

3.3.2 Cancellation Policy Generalizations

Chose a policy which is equitable for teacher and student. Your time is as important as your student's. Try to prevent extra bookkeeping work or modifying your schedule simply because a student canceled their lesson for a personal reason such as a trip to the mall or movie.

In-home studios have the option of not dealing with weather issues. Use this location to your advantage by not canceling in bad weather. Do not make the studio cancellation policy so stringent that you haven't allowed yourself the option of an occasional missed lesson.

3.4 Summary

Three important aspects to consider once a business plan and curricular concerns have been addressed are scheduling, tuition, and cancellation policies.

Establish and post business hours once you have determined how much time and which days will be devoted to this enterprise. In less densely populated areas, community and school schedules will need to be taken into account. Some adults and home-schooled students could be taught earlier in the day while working people and school-age youngsters will need a later slot. Determine what breaks in the schedule you will personally require. List hours on all mailings and studio information.

Do not waiver from your schedule for a bold parent who insists that their child can only attend lessons on a day that you do not teach.

Refer to lesson charges as "tuition." Several factors need to be contemplated when deciding what the tuition will be: instructor credentials, studio location, expenses, as well as length and type of lesson provided. Additional fees may need to be charged including: materials, fees to cover overhead and supplies, recital fees, or book, music, and methods materials fees. Determine when and how these fees will be collected, be it weekly, monthly, or by the semester/term.

Every studio must deal with cancellations. Establish a workable policy and adhere to it.

Practical Application

1. Call schools in your area and find out when the school day is finished.

2. Establish a practical teaching schedule for yourself deciding upon lesson length and length of teaching day. List reasoning for your scheduling selections.

3. Research local private instruction prices. What is the average?

4. Go online and research cancellation policies from across the country.

5. Write your own lesson payment and cancellation policies in a clear and concise manner. List reasoning for your pricing and cancellation policies.

CHAPTER 4

Location, Location, Location!

4.1 Selecting a Location for Instruction

When final decisions have been made regarding lesson dynamics, continue realizing the case statement by determining a location for the music instruction to take place. Instructors who are establishing their first studio or relocating may consult the Independent Teacher Location Information Service. This directory can be found on the Music Teachers National Association website (www.mtna.org) and provides a listing of areas in the United States where quality independent music teachers are needed and where they already exist. Also, the Internet is an accurate and obvious source for determining if there is an instruction facility in your area. Look in the Yellow Pages under music instruction to assess the competition and level of saturation in an area. Remember that the listings in the Yellow Pages are storefront locations and will not give the number of instructors offering in-home instruction. The number of private instructors can only be determined when you are knowledgeable of an area.

Once the city, town, or neighborhood for the studio is decided upon, there are four options for the exact locale for teaching your lessons. These options include:
- **instructor's home**
- **alternate location**
- **student's home**
- **existing business owned by someone else**

Pros and cons are associated with each of these locations. Study the suggestions in this chapter to aid in the decision as to which location will best suit your individual needs.

4.2 In-Home Studio Zoning

Before deciding upon an in-home studio, it is necessary to consult local zoning ordinances to see if an in-home business is feasible in your area. Many cities and counties have provisions in place for in-home businesses. As of 2002, Michigan is the only state in the United States that protects in-home music instruction from local zoning laws.

A highly-publicized zoning dispute in DeKalb County Georgia regarding an in-home studio was settled with an ordinance which now allows in-home instruction. Music teachers in DeKalb County are now considered an "educational service," which means they will not need a business license. It seems the key in this case is for music teachers to define themselves as an educational service rather than a business.

Knowing your legal rights may save time, will definitely save effort and worry, and ultimately may save money. Do not rely on the advice or opinion of a realtor, relative, colleague, or friend as fact. Consult the local government and/or legal council for knowledge of community ordinances regarding licensing and zoning issues. The legal council most knowledgeable in this area would be a "land-use" attorney. However, a local zoning or planning board should be able to provide answers to any zoning questions. The city government will have a zoning department which will supply all requested information. Copies of applicable ordinances can also be found at the local library. These documents will provide the necessary information regarding the legality of running an in-home business.

It is also suggested that any covenant that may be enacted by a neighborhood association be checked.

Consider these preliminary steps when planning your in-home studio:
• Look for a neighborhood which has been zoned commercial or a combination commercial/residential. Older neighborhoods are more likely to be zoned as commercial.
• Review the deeds, records, and zoning laws before purchasing or renting a new home in which a studio may be housed.
• Talk to future neighbors to gauge their receptiveness to having an in-home music studio in such close proximity to their residence.
• Apply for any licenses necessary to open the in-home business.

Many areas have existing legislature making home instruction legal; however, violation of noise or traffic ordinances could generate a citation and ultimately close the business. This is why it is very important to talk with and have congenial relationships with neighbors. Some of the concerns that neighbors will voice will deal with noise, safety for children as heightened traffic is introduced, and parking concerns. Be prepared for dealing with these complaints. Assure neighbors that you will make every effort to control these issues.

If existing laws conflict with and restrict the studio, it may be possible for a zoning board to approve a variance. Consider hiring legal council to aid in this scenario.

Practical Application

Use your current home address as a possible location to research. If this address is not feasible (if you are college student living in a dorm, for instance), use a former address or select a random address from the phone book.

Contact the local government or check at the local library to research zoning issues. Are there any restrictions, laws, or guidelines that will affect your business? Consider the following areas:
- zoning ordinances
- parking restrictions
- noise restrictions
- grandfather clauses
- sign ordinances
- entrance requirements

Are there any unusual circumstances that may affect your business?

Upon completion of your research, write a brief feasibility study that includes any legal issues that may affect or interfere with your location selection.

4.3 In-Home Studio

There are many advantages to having an in-home business. The greatest advantage is financial, followed closely by convenience. Generally, the financial pluses are plentiful regarding tax issues (tax issues will be fully addressed in Chapter 9). The attractiveness of working at home also increases as travel and fuel prices escalate. The negatives that transpire for an in-home business stem primarily from the loss of privacy. Your home will become a public place and lifestyle must be adjusted to the flow of traffic through your personal space. Other negatives deal with the public perception of an in-home studio.

4.3.1 Parking

Specific provisions for ample parking should be made for studio patrons. Many parents with students under the age of 16 will opt to wait in the waiting area, but even more will stay in their car during lesson time. These parents will need a specific place to park. Regardless of whether the parking option is on the street, in a public lot, parking garage, or in the driveway, a designated location for the vehicles of your patrons is a necessary convenience. Mention of the designated location should be made to new students at enrollment and should become an automatic part of your introductory case statement information shared with new patrons.

If parking is limited, consider asking parents to drop off and pick up their children rather than remaining parked. If this provision is necessary, set up a routine phone conference or regularly email these parents since they will seldom be seen in person. Caution students to avoid parking in other residents' parking spaces. Your car should be out of the way so that patrons have the closest parking options.

If space permits, offer a handicapped parking spot.

4.3.2 Handicap Accessibility

An in-home business is subject to "public accommodation" provisions of the Americans with Disabilities Act (ADA). The ADA prohibits discrimination by public accommodations. Places of public accommodation include locations such as malls, churches, restaurants, schools, parks, and museums. Barrier removal and alterations need only be accomplished when it is "readily achievable" to do so. This means "easy to achieve without much difficulty or expense."

Achievable modifications to an in-home studio might include:
- Keep steps to a minimum wherever possible.
- Install hand rails at all steps.
- Install a simple ramp.
- Improve doorway width. Take doors off hinges, if necessary, to make rooms accessible to a wheelchair (the average wheel chair needs a minimum 32-inch opening).

Modifications for handicapped students that would fundamentally alter the nature of the teaching services provided are not required by law. For example, you may legally decline to accept a blind student because you cannot provide the teaching method required to instruct this student. It has been the author's experience, however, that putting forth the extra effort to accommodate handicapped students will be personally rewarding for both student and teacher.

4.3.3 Private Entrance

Whenever possible, the student entrance should be separate from the personal/private home entrance. The more separation that exists between the private and public use of the home, the more professional the business will be perceived by the patrons. This may also be a required specification in local zoning. Upon enrollment, inform the student of the specific door to use for entering and exiting the in-home studio by including this in case statement information.

The Private Music Instruction Manual: A Guide for the Independent Music Educator • Rebecca Osborn

Keep the walkways leading to the entrance clear of snow, ice, dirt, and children's toys. Strive to make the entrance professional and aesthetically pleasing.

4.3.4 Waiting Area

A waiting area should be made available for parents and students whenever possible. This area should be a comfortable, clean, educational environment. If at all feasible, the waiting area for the in-home studio should not be used by family members (including pets) during business hours.

Waiting Area Considerations

Flooring

The flooring in the waiting area will experience a high degree of "wear and tear." Dirt, mud, water, sand, leaves, and anything else that travels on children's feet will come into the waiting room, studio, and home. Durable floor mats and area rugs are ideal and necessary to protect the existing flooring. A separate mat is needed at the main entrance.

Seating

Some sort of seating should be offered. Look for economical and sturdy seating that can withstand varied sizes of patrons as well as varied levels of cleanliness. Students may come directly from a ball practice with no time for clean-up.

Outerwear Storage

Provisions should be made for the placement and storage of coats, jackets, hats, gloves, umbrellas, and wet shoes. Place hooks at child and adult heights.

Bulletin Board

The waiting area should be used as the place to post announcements that are pertinent to studio patrons. Items to consider posting include:
- news items pertaining to studio dates/events, changes/cancellations, and policies.
- newspaper clippings about students.
- lesson schedule.
- area auditions and performing opportunities.
- birthdays and celebrations of students.

Reading Materials

Include books with educational value as options for reading materials offered in the waiting room. Order magazine subscriptions (tax deductible) that are appropriate for students and their families. There are many choices available so have fun making this selection.

Offer pamphlets or newspapers of local educational interest. Is there a children's museum in the area? Are there local play groups for preschool age children? Are there area community theatres? Post flyers for local music stores, tuners, and technicians. Is there an area children's choir or youth orchestra? Obtain information from these organizations and offer their pamphlets, brochures, and press releases as reading material in the waiting area.

Secure information, printings, and pamphlets from music education organizations via mail or web such as:
- American Music Conference
- Music Achievement Council
- Music Teachers National Association
- Music Educators National Conference

Possible educational books of interest to your patrons to have in the waiting area might include:
- *The Mozart Effect* by Don Campbell
- *Introduction to the Musical Brain* by Don Campbell
- *Art, Mind, and Brain* by Howard Gardner
- *Good Music, Brighter Children: Simple and Practical Ideas to Help Transform Your Child's Life Through the Power of Music* by Sharlene Habermeyer
- *Teaching and Learning through Multiple Intelligences* by Lois Choksy

These books describe and inform on topics dealing with the intellectual and creative benefits of music education. The information presented in these writings documents the benefits of music education which are widely known by music educators, but are not always known to the general public.

You should be knowledgeable regarding books, musical pamphlets, and any periodicals that are kept in the waiting room and be able to discuss them if needed.

Puzzles and Games

A correlation has been verified between music and spatial learning. Puzzles serve to ready the brain for music instruction. There are countless puzzles and games available at educational toy stores and on the web. These do not necessarily need to be music related. Children and adults alike will respond to puzzles. Puzzles are also a good opportunity to let parents know some of the brain research that has taken place.

Studio Photo Album

Consider compiling a photo album with pictures of students at lessons and in performance. Have the album available for viewing in the waiting area.

TV/VCR

Television is not a necessity in a waiting room. If a TV is in your waiting area, consider purchasing a VCR as well so that educational and music videos can be played and viewed by students. Do not allow students to make viewing choices.

Computer

If a computer is available, offer music games and instructional tools for students to use in the waiting room (see software options listed in Chapter 2).

Payment Drop Box

Display a drop box in the waiting room. This may be locked if necessary. This drop box, besides looking official, is a handy way to collect tuition when you're teaching or when you are not open for business. Encourage and urge parents and students to use the drop box method for payment as it doesn't take valuable lesson time to deal with payment issues. There will occasionally be that parent who says, "I didn't pay because you were teaching, and I didn't want to interrupt you." A drop box will eliminate this excuse for late payments.

4.3.5 Restroom

Restroom facilities should be clean and well stocked with paper and cleaning products. Consider making personal health articles available for the occasional emergencies which require a band aid, aspirin, or feminine hygiene item. A plunger is also a good investment.

4.3.6 Teaching Facility

This is a room that should reflect your personality as well as practicality. The aesthetics and mood that you create in the teaching facility itself are very important. You will spend a large amount of time in this room. Make it your domain. Obviously, a professional look will lend to the creditability of the studio. Consider decorating in a student friendly manner, that will inspire and relax children and adults alike.

- The studio should be well lit with additional lighting such as stand, piano, and floor lighting used in conjunction with traditional overhead lighting.
- A large mirror is a near necessity.
- Make acoustics a consideration whenever possible. Place pianos on outside walls or where the sound will move to areas of the building causing the least disturbance. Thick carpeting and doors will help encase sound. Dropped ceilings with acoustic tiles as well as fabric on the walls can aid in the muffling of sound if needed. Keep windows closed during lesson times to keep sound heard by the neighbors to a minimum.

The studios should be easily accessible to parents. In these times when the headlines are full of teachers, coaches, scout leaders, and adults in leadership positions who are not above reproach, it is a good idea for the studio to have an open-door policy. Parents have entrusted their greatest treasure to your keeping and they deserve 100% confidence regarding the safety of their children in your charge. If you are going to teach behind a closed door, consider putting a window in the door or using a French door. Let parents know they are welcome to attend lessons at any time. If acoustics allow, keep the door ajar.

Have water available in the studio. It is a necessity, not only for your teaching, but also for the students. If the rental of a water machine is not financially possible, keep a pitcher of ice water and cups centrally located for students, parents, and yourself.

Ventilation is something to consider. A lesson will generate body heat. Have a fan conveniently located.

The Private Music Instruction Manual: A Guide for the Independent Music Educator • Rebecca Osborn

4.3.7 It's a Family Business

There are members of the public who believe that since your time is spent at home, you are not really working. They do not understand that working at home is work. They may even resent when you decline chaperoning a field trip, attending a daytime meeting, or leading a scout troupe. This misconceived attitude may also be held by family members. The family perception might be that since you are at home, then certainly you can fulfill at least some home responsibilities. Allow the family to be part of the in-home business planning process. Let them see how comprehensive this business is and how life-altering this business can and will be. Share expectations with family members regarding chores, behavior, and time management in an in-home business.

4.3.8 The White Glove Test

Cleanliness is of prime importance for the in-home business. Your professional image will be visibly presented in your home. Check for what a student will see, hear, and smell. Make sure personal items, children's toys, and unsightly clutter are behind closed doors. Are there cooking or pet odors? Ask a trusted and honest friend if the smell of your house is pleasant. Use air fresheners and fragrant candles during non-business hours. Keep family pets out of the public area as they produce odors. Also, many people have pet allergies and will be bothered by the presence of a pet. If the family area must be used as a public area for either the waiting room, studio, or both, and there is a family pet who frequents this area, make certain this is mentioned to a prospective student at the time of the inquiry call in the event that they have any allergies.

4.3.9 Public Perception

Some people will feel that since a business is in the home, it is less professional and therefore does not need to adhere to policies and procedures that have been established. There is a general feeling that lessons should be at bargain basement prices and that students can make demands on your time since you are "already at home." This problem will have to be dealt with by all in-home music instructors.

4.3.10 Advantages and Disadvantages

> **In-Home Studio**
>
> **Advantages**
> - There are no travel expenses.
> - There is no travel time.
> - There are many tax benefits (see Chapter 9) including mortgage/rent, utilities, insurance, *etc.*
> - Additional curriculum offerings can be made available, especially associated with technology.
>
> **Disadvantages**
> - Privacy is lost.
> - Expenses for maintenance of home, insurance, *etc.* increase.

Practical Applications

Write a teacher personality/lifestyle profile to help you determine your feelings about an in-home teaching situation.

List three personality/lifestyle traits that will conflict with the in-home instruction location.

1. _____

2. _____

3. _____

List three personality/lifestyle traits that will coexist harmoniously with the in-home instruction location.

1. _____

2. _____

3. _____

Which list best describes you?

Do you feel that an in-home teaching situation is an alternative that you should investigate? Why or why not?

4.4 Alternate Location

If results from the personality/lifestyle evaluation lead you to believe that an in-home teaching facility isn't preferred or feasible, then an alternate location must be selected.

An alternate location used for private music teaching that is not a personal residence would be a location such as a storefront, church, school, day-care center, community center, the local Y, or another person's home. These areas can be rented or purchased. This could also be an existing music business in which you join the staff and rent instructional space.

As far as the public is concerned, a non-residence site lends instant professionalism to instruction. There seems to be a sense in public opinion that teaching in the home is not as professional or the instructor isn't as knowledgeable as those teaching in an outside location. Obviously, the chosen curriculum, instructor credentials, or teaching techniques will be identical, regardless of location. Unfortunately, patrons often disagree. Therefore, this public perception may produce an advantage in the numbers of students enrolled.

Many prospective alternate facilities are eager to support the arts and will support music instruction as a welcome addition to their offerings. In order to achieve more commercial success in an out-of-home location, develop curriculum additions that are complimentary to the facility.

Church	*offer sacred music*
Pre-school	*offer lessons to toddlers*
School	*offer age-appropriate lessons*
Community Center	*offer lessons to seniors or other specific groups that the center would encourage*

Also consider using a student's home as a studio location. Perhaps a student lives in a geographic area that is more conveniently located for public access. Perhaps this student has a professional studio atmosphere in their home that proves to be ideal for in-home lessons. Strike a barter, or pay rent to the owners if they are willing to accept liability and are interested in this arrangement. **Secure a written contract before entering into this or any similar relationship.**

4.4.1 Professional Appearance

Many of the considerations for an alternate location such as parking, entrance, handicap accessibility, and restrooms will be under the jurisdiction of the owner of the facility and are not your responsibility. Be aware of cleanliness and general maintenance of the facility as it will serve as a reflection of the business. A professional music instruction business  must be in a professional location. If the public areas are not clean and well maintained, the location will imply your lack of professionalism to the public eye. Don't sign any type of rental agreement without 100% confidence and satisfaction in the facility and its care and maintenance.

4.4.2 Individual Studio

The appearance of the studio is a primary responsibility of the instructor. A bulletin board should be in a place of prominence so it can be viewed by all students. As in the in-home studio, this location should be used as a place to make announcements that are pertinent to studio patrons. The teaching facility should be aesthetically pleasing and reflect the instructor's personality. Be aware of lighting and supply a mirror and water for the students if at all possible. If there is a locked area or location where materials can be kept secure, it might be easier to use this location rather than transport materials from home to work on a weekly/daily basis.

4.4.3 Acoustics

Make sure the location is acoustically appropriate. Consider the possibility of a teacher using a preschool facility as their studio. Imagine trying to teach a private lesson while twenty-two four-year-olds have play time in the next room. In this case, acoustics in conjunction with scheduling are of utmost importance.

4.4.4 Rental Agreement

Look carefully at whatever rental agreement is offered by this location. Your rent serves as assurance that a safe and professional appearance will be maintained. Make sure the agreement shows the liability which will be incurred by the facility if injury should take place. In the event that a contract is not offered, (at a church or student's home for example) you will need to take the initiative to secure legal assistance for the writing of a rental agreement or contract.

4.4.5 Advantages and Disadvantages

Alternate Location

Advantages
- The facility owner will assume liability responsibility and not the individual teacher.
- Facility maintenance and cleanliness is the responsibility of the facility owner.
- There is less financial commitment for studio setup.
- There will be some tax deductions (see Chapter 9).

Disadvantages
- There will be a monthly rental payment due or a percentage of your earnings required by the property owner.
- There may be scheduling constraints.
- There is travel time.
- There is travel expense.
- You must travel with instructional materials.
- Technology offerings additional to the curriculum may not be an option.

Practical Application

Write a teacher personality/lifestyle profile to help you determine your feelings about teaching in an alternate instruction location.

List three personality/lifestyle traits that will conflict with the alternate instruction location.

1. _____

2. _____

3. _____

List three personality/lifestyle traits that will coexist harmoniously with the alternate instruction location.

1. _____

2. _____

3. _____

Which list best describes you?

Do you feel that teaching at an alternate location is an option that you should investigate? Why or why not?

4.5 Itinerate Lessons

Itinerant lessons (traveling and teaching at a students' home) are a third option for your instruction location.

4.5.1 Traveling Teacher

The one word that describes success in this type of teaching environment is ORGANIZATION. Develop a system to check for all necessary items that are needed for each and every lesson (see Chapter 5). Nothing is worse than knowing exactly how and what is needed to teach only to discover that the necessary materials are not on hand.

Keep method books, theory texts and manipulatives, equipment (such as valve oil, portable music stands, strings, guitar tuners, *etc.*), and other regularly needed materials readily available.

4.5.2 The Teaching Room

If teaching piano lessons, the location of the piano will dictate where in the student's home the lesson will take place. Otherwise, the best location will need to be selected. Family rooms, livings rooms, or home offices are good choices for a teaching location in a student's home.

While parents should be encouraged to attend this lesson, siblings can be extremely distracting and probably should be prohibited from the lesson. The same is true for the family pet. Make sure that a student knows that they will not be accepting phone calls during their lesson time.

4.5.3 Advantages and Disadvantages

Itinerate Lessons

Advantages
- There is no need to purchase location liability insurance.
- There is no need for facility maintenance and cleanliness to be a consideration.
- There is less financial commitment as there is no facility setup.
- There is no rent paid.
- There will be tax deductions (see Chapter 9).
- This type of lesson is considered very attractive to many patrons.

Disadvantages
- There will be in-home teaching distractions.
- There is travel time.
- There is travel expense.
- There is a burden of traveling with all equipment.
- This type of lesson is not considered very professional to many patrons.
- Technology curriculum will not likely be available.
- These lessons are very difficult to keep on schedule.

Practical Application

Write a teacher personality/lifestyle profile to help you determine your feelings about itinerate teaching.

List three personality/lifestyle traits that will conflict with the itinerate instruction location.

1. _____

2. _____

3. _____

List 3 personality/lifestyle traits that will coexist harmoniously with the itinerate instruction location.

1. _____

2. _____

3. _____

Which list best describes you?

Do you feel itinerate music instruction is an alternative that you should investigate? Why or why not?

4.6 Existing Business Owned by Someone Else

Some private music instructors choose to teach at an existing instructional facility and to be on the staff of another person's studio. You'll be considered an independent contractor by the government. The studio will charge rent for the use of the facility but they will take the risks by supplying location, advertising, and insurance. The majority of studios expect the instructor to supply all materials needed for instruction and they often require instructors to collect all tuition and fees. Therefore, this scenario is similar to that of a traveling teacher.

Study the studio contract carefully. Know what is expected both financially and legally. If a contract is not required, perhaps you should worry.

Existing Business Lessons

Advantages
- There is no need to purchase location liability insurance.
- There is no need for facility maintenance and cleanliness to be a responsibility.
- There is less financial commitment.
- There will be tax deductions (see Chapter 9).
- This type of lesson is considered very professional to many patrons.

Disadvantages
- There is rent to be paid.
- There is travel time.
- There is travel expense.
- There is a burden of traveling with all equipment.

4.7 Final Selection

Upon looking at the four possible locations for instruction options offered in this chapter, chose the one for which you would be best suited. Look at location thoughtfully. Don't spend a great deal of money setting up the ideal in-home studio if you'll be moving within a year. Do you believe your decision will still fit you five years from now? Ten years from now? What changes do you project during that time period?

4.8 Summary

It is important to select an easily accessible location for your studio. Options include your home, student's home, an established music instruction business or an alternate location.

If a home studio is selected, be sure to research local zoning ordinances for feasibility. Knowing your legal rights will save time, money, and worry. Neighborhood associations also need to be investigated, and it is advisable to talk to neighbors. Provide for ample parking, and consider handicap accessibility (checking once again on legalities). If possible, the entrance for students should be separate from the family entrance with the provision of a waiting area for students and parents. The home should be comfortable, clean, well-lit, well-ventilated, and not used by the family during business hours. Consider needs such as seating, coat racks, adequately supplied rest room, reading materials, *etc*. To facilitate tuition payments, provide a locked payment drop box in the waiting room.

Educate family members as well as the public to seriously regard this endeavor as a business. How you approach it will be a key factor in their perception.

If a home studio is not workable, it may be best to select an alternate location such as a storefront, church, community center, or students' homes. An existing music instruction business may be an excellent choice eliminating some of the problems encountered in other locations. Be sure any agreements made are written, legal, and signed.

Practical Application:

Select a location for your studio that best suits you and your student's needs. Be sure you are knowledgeable about the legal requirements of any location you choose.

List at least five reasons for your location.

CHAPTER 5
Equipment & Supplies

5.1 Equipment Needs

As the case statement for your independent music instruction business continues to be realized, the need will arise to purchase equipment and supplies. Obviously, the amount of equipment and number of supplies necessary will be parallel with the intended scope of the business as well as its location. Regardless of whether the studio is in your personal residence or an alternate location, many of the same items and equipment will need to be secured.

Some may remember the "traveling" music teachers in grade school. These were the teachers who carried their entire music program on a wheeled audio/visual cart from classroom to classroom. This may be similar to what you experience. Music, metronome, amplification equipment, valve oil, and your instrument are just a few of the items you may need with you at all times. Now is the time to organize it all.

5.2 Studio Office

Regardless of which location you select for your business, you will need a studio office or business area in which to collect and organize all records. Any well-run business has a headquarters. Your studio office will serve as the headquarters for your studio. When income is involved, paperwork is a necessity. Your studio office will serve as the structural home for the paperwork that is necessary for your business endeavor. Even if your studio is not in your home, it is often easiest for your studio office to be in your home.

Your studio office should house:
- computer
- telephone, voicemail system or answering machine, fax machine
- contact telephone numbers
- adding machine
- copier
- tax records and files
- business receipts
- mileage records
- attendance records
- payment records
- business supplies
- postage supplies
- music and student files

Ideally, your studio office will be equipped with a private phone line used specifically for the business.

If an individual line is out of the question, investigate a phone that will have a ring that sounds unlike the home phone line. Also, consider purchasing an answering machine that has separate "mailboxes" so that one can be specifically set up for the business and a second one set up for home and personal use. Instruct family members to allow the answering machine to always pick up the phone, or to always answer the home phone with the name of the business. Remember that a primary goal is to present your business to the public in the most professional manner possible. A proper answer on the answering machine or voicemail system will help you achieve the professionalism you are seeking.

5.3 Necessary Studio Equipment and Supplies

Below you will find an alphabetical list of equipment and supplies necessary for all facets of private music instruction. The equipment is divided by teaching location.

	In-Home Studio	Alternate Location	Student Home	Studio Office
amplification Amplification is used in guitar instruction or to practice for a live venue.	•	•	•	
answering machine/voicemail This is the most efficient and professional way to respond to an inquiry.				•
bathroom supplies This would include tissue, toilet paper, pain reliever, hand soap, nail clippers, band aids, disinfectant, a plunger, and feminine hygiene products. Tissue should be available in the waiting room, restroom, and studio.	•			
binder/planner/handheld computer Keep a log of all students which includes all personal information as well as notes regarding payment and literature assigned and needed. The information kept in this location can later be transferred to the business computer if need be.	•	•	•	
blank tapes It may be necessary to record rehearsal tapes, or you may wish to tape the lesson.	•	•	•	
brief case/book bag Find one that offers the most efficient way to take music from one location to another. This should offer protection from the elements as well as storage for all the other items that are necessary for your teaching.		•	•	

	In-Home Studio	Alternate Location	Student Home	Studio Office
calculator Use a calculator for quick and accurate calculations.	•	•	•	•
CD/tape player There are very few tape recorders currently available that have built-in microphones. The most reliable source for this equipment seems to be online vendors. At this time, Sony and Panasonic both manufacture models that offer suitable quality for your recording needs at an economical price. There are currently some combination CD/tape players with built-in microphones, but they seem to have very poor quality.	•	•	•	
clock Find a clock with easily read, highly visible numbers. A second hand is sometimes needed for timing purposes. Also, timeliness is highly appreciated by both the coming and the departing student. Always make every effort to keep lessons on time.	•			
computer Invest in an application such as *Quicken* to keep all receipts and business expenses. This will serve to expedite completion of tax forms as well as keep an accurate assessment of how much money the business is making. Also keep student records which include contact, payment, and attendance information. There are companies which offer software specifically geared toward lesson organization, or develop a customized database using an application such as *Access* or *FileMaker Pro*.	•	•	•	•
coat/wall hooks Put these at appropriate heights for students to leave book bags, coats, hats, and umbrellas.	•			
copier This will be helpful for the business. Be aware of copyright laws and appropriate uses of a copier.				•
dry erase teaching board This is helpful tool and more fun to use than a piece of paper and pencil. Look for laptop sizes that have staff, keyboard, or fret boards already printed on them. If using an in-home studio, leave enough wall space to place a dry erase board in the teaching area so it can be used frequently.	•	•	•	
fax machine This is especially helpful if you have a wholesale account at a music publishing house or distributor. Most of these companies offer a greater percentage discount on faxed orders.				•

	In-Home Studio	Alternate Location	Student Home	Studio Office
fan Private lessons tend to produce body heat.	•			
floor mats/area rugs Will help to control the dirt tracked into your home.	•			
ink/toner cartridges Necessary for copier, printer, and fax machine.				•
instrument for instruction Don't forget the obvious.	•	•	•	
magazines for waiting area This business expense for your waiting room is appreciated by your patrons and their family members.	•			
metronome Small electronic ones are reliable, efficient, and save space.	•	•	•	
microphone This is helpful for teaching microphone technique and for recording purposes.	•			
microphone stand This is helpful in teaching microphone technique as well.	•			
mileage log This in needed for tax purposes and should be kept where it will be easily available to you.		•	•	
money drop box This is helpful for students to leave payments when you are teaching so as not to disturb your lesson and get you off schedule.	•			
music library Your music library should be selected considering available space and how far and how often the library must travel.	•	•	•	
music/folding stand Invest in a quality stand as it will be used every day that you teach (except piano instructors).	•	•	•	
office supplies Pens, pencils, stapler, and scissors are all needed occasionally.	•	•	•	•
printer Use to generate your original business and pedagogical materials.				•
piano/keyboard Helpful to have to teach theory concepts.	•			

The Private Music Instruction Manual: A Guide for the Independent Music Educator • Rebecca Osborn

	In-Home Studio	Alternate Location	Student Home	Studio Office
phone An individual phone line for the business makes for a very professional presentation to the public.				•
prize/incentives Gifts and stickers may make the difference in whether or not a student practices. Some educators disagree with the use of incentives, however, many students expect and respond well to them.	•	•	•	
storage/filing system Music, student files, text books, workbooks, tax papers, copies of bills, and insurance policies are just some of the items that should be stored.	•	•	•	•
tools Tools needed to adjust and repair your instrument are important to have available.	•	•	•	
TV/VCR Some students will feel more comfortable waiting for their lesson if a television is available.	•			

5.4 Necessary Printing and Paper Products

Along with the equipment that is necessary for private music instruction, there are many paper product needs as well. Many of these items are related to advertising and will be discussed fully in Chapter 6. However, the remainder of these items are necessary for the day-to-day running of your business.

	In-Home Studio	Alternate Location	Student Home	Studio Office
achievement awards If you design a logo specifically for the business, use this logo on computer generated certificates and awards. Many companies offer awards that come in packages of 20-25 certificates for a very reasonable price. Offer awards for anything you think should be recognized, and don't forget rewarding good and consistent practice.	•	•	•	•
birthday cards When a student signs up for lessons, ask his/her birthday. Even adults like to get cards. Young children will be especially be excited about receiving a birthday card. Personalized musical birthday cards with your business name or logo are a great public relations opportunity as well as a plain old thoughtful gesture.	•	•	•	•
brochures It is important to have a well-designed, computer-generated brochure that describes everything about you and your business to the public.	•	•	•	•
business cards Don't ever be without your business cards. You never know who you'll meet, and you should be prepared.	•	•	•	•
gift certificates Selling gift certificates is a great way to help others encourage your students. They are especially effective around holidays.	•	•	•	•
logo design stationery Professional looking stationery should be used for all correspondence.	•	•	•	•
newsletter It's always difficult to stay in contact with all of your students. Use either a traditional mailing or an email format to contact students and their families. This is a great time to let them know what you're doing, if you have any upcoming special events, and any general announcements.	•	•	•	•

	In-Home Studio	Alternate Location	Student Home	Studio Office
phone inquiry sheet Have a sheet available for family members or for anyone else who may help you by answering your phone. In the event that someone else fields a phone call for you, use these to keep track of interested persons who call. It is also helpful for you to have a record of any phone conversation you may have had with a prospective student. If they have follow-up questions and call again, or if they call back to sign up for lessons with you, it's good for you to have the notes from your previous conversation in hand.	•	•	•	•
practice logs If don't like using stock lesson assignment books, then design a personalized assignment sheet and copy it for all of your students.	•	•	•	•
return address label or stamp This looks very professional for minimal expense and will save the time it takes to hand write a return address label.	•	•	•	•
sign This is only necessary if you have a store front location. Remember to check the local ordinances which may influence size and placement of a sign on the storefront.	•	•	•	•

5.5 Business Computer Needs

Use your computer for your business. Many of the necessary items for instruction and organization already suggested in this chapter will be created and stored on your computer. As with all other important computer information, always back up all of your files.

When selecting a computer, software, and additional peripherals, make sure you choose the right tools for the job of running your business. First consider what type of machine would work the best for your situation: a laptop you can carry with you or a desktop which you will use in only one location.

The basic software you will need will include the following:

- word processing for correspondence (*i.e.* Microsoft *Word, AppleWorks*)
- database for keeping records (*i.e. FileMaker Pro,* Microsoft *Access*)
- email for communication (*i.e.* Microsoft *Outlook,* Microsoft *Entourage*)
- web browser for placing online orders (*i.e.* Microsoft *Internet Explorer,* Netscape *Communicator,* Apple *Safari*)
- financial software for keeping business records (*i.e. Quicken, MYOB*)

Of course, depending on your level of computer experience, you may wish to move beyond the basics. You may consider the purchase of more sophisticated page layout and design software for flyers and mailings. You may also consider finding a web host and developing a web page for your business for the purpose of public relations and communication. Photos from a digital camera can be used to document performances for your studio scrapbook or to include on web pages. A handheld computer such as a Palm can help you keep track of your student contact information, your teaching schedule, and mileage and expenses with the software that is included. The possibilities are limitless.

5.5.1 Student Database

Develop a database and keep a record of each of your students. The information incorporated and maintained on each student should include:

- student name
- parent name
- address
- phone
- student birthday
- payment received
- attendance dates
- books ordered/received/paid
- a section for notes to describe assignment

5.5.2 Music Library Database

Create a database for the music in your library. If you plan to have extra music on hand so that you or the student do not need to make a hurried trip to the store, keep a record using a database. These records will make the monthly trip to the music store easier, and you will have an accurate record of this valuable asset.

Also, keep a database of music you own. This database is especially helpful for replacement situations and for insurance purposes. If a student loses a book you loan them from your library, this will make replacement simple.

5.6 Library Needs

Every music library should include some basic materials:

Extra copies of the method books you use
Sometimes a student may forget their assigned materials. Have extras on hand for such occasions.

Sight reading materials
Try to include sight reading in every lesson. Varied materials should be available offering differing technical aspects as well as keys and tempos. While a student is waiting, he or she could be studying a piece to be sightread for the upcoming lesson.

Technique materials
Have technique materials readily available for technical needs (*e.g.* the Vaccai method). For example, if a vocalist has an assigned piece of literature which presents a melisma that they are having trouble mastering, have technical studies materials available that can be borrowed from your studio library that will assist the student in the technical proficiency of melismas.

Music dictionary
Have a dictionary available in case you run across an editor's term or a composer with whom you are unfamiliar.

Staff paper
Have blank staff paper available for demonstrations, assignments, or for teaching music theory concepts.

Music publisher catalogs
All of the major publishing houses have catalogs that are available to teachers. Contact them and place your name on their mailing list. Locate the name of the publisher of your favorite series of instructional materials. Find their website and let them know of your interest. They will add you to their mailing list and contact you when they have new issues and may even send complimentary materials.

Websites
Maintain a list of useful websites that you can suggest to students for further reference. If you have a website for your studio, include these on a Links page.

The Private Music Instruction Manual: A Guide for the Independent Music Educator • Rebecca Osborn

5.7 Summary

Your equipment needs will be determined in part by the scope and location of your business. It will be necessary to secure and organize necessary items to be used.

Regardless of location, you will need an office area in which to assemble and organize all records and files which must be maintained on a current basis. If possible, have a private business phone line.

Use your computer for your business. Many necessary items for instruction and organization can be created and stored in your computer. Be sure to back up all your files. Develop a database and keep a record of each student.

Create another database for music in your library. Needs for a music library include extra copies of the methods books used, sight-reading materials, technique materials, a music dictionary, staff paper, and music publishing catalogues.

Practical Application

1. Select one of the possible studio locations. Make a needs list specifically tailored for that studio.

2. Generate a needs list for your office.

3. Note the items you already own on your needs list.

4. Prioritize the items in order of need.

5. Purchase the items allowed by your budget.

CHAPTER 6
It Pays to Advertise

6.1 Target the Audience

In order for an independent music business to receive a successful response from the local public, some form of advertising is required. Advertisement can be on as small or large a scale as budget and desire for business growth dictate. There are independent studio instructors in the United States who make comfortable six figure incomes solely from their teaching. There are independent studio instructors in the U.S. who make several hundred dollars a month in order to supplement their primary income. The ultimate financial desire and time commitment will determine the advertising budget of the business.

Since the budget of many teachers is limited, the ideas offered here are generally frugal in nature. This chapter will present some of the varied marketing alternatives that are available as well as offer guidance regarding how and when to make advertising investments.

This chapter offers a series of advertising ideas that will help to formulate the plan to attract students. Select the ideas that seem to best fit the studio budget and your personality.

At this point, it has already been established which instrument will be taught and where the teaching will occur. Now it is time to target the studio's students. The specific instructional offerings will dictate the advertisement style and location used to attract students. If the studio specialty is beginning Suzuki violin, then the targeted market is preschools and elementary schools in areas that have a string program. If the studio specialty is jazz guitar, then the focus market should be guitar shops, the local high school, and night spots that showcase jazz talent.

A demographic break-down can be purchased from several online services. This analysis presents the population age, income, education, and other pertinent information regarding the persons in a specific geographic area. Demographics data can aid in targeting the market in a given area. They pinpoint where to send a mass mailing, which newspaper to use for press releases and print advertisements, as well as which grocery stores are the best ones for flyer placement. If the use of demographics is too specific or costly, use logic and common sense to decide how to target possible students who fit the studio offerings. For instance, a retirement

community would not be a good advertising venue to find new Kindermusik students unless aimed at grandparents who oversee and supplement the education of their grandchildren.

6.2 Initial Advertising Expenditures

Initial marketing costs may be higher than the budgeted projected monthly expenditures. These expenses should be viewed as necessary start-up costs as well as an investment in the business. After all, without students, there is no teaching. Advertising is the primary way to attract students. Eventually, the business will maintain the necessary student population because the reputation of the studio will be fueled by word of mouth recommendations. Until that level of recognition is achieved, advertising is a necessity and should be budgeted accordingly.

Suggested resources for locating national media would include such books as:

- *The Standard Periodical Directory* which lists newspapers, magazines, radio and TV stations throughout the country.
- *The Media Factbook,* which is updated annually and published by your local United Way. At a cost of $10-15, it's a sound investment.

From a marketing/advertising prospective, if your annual projected revenue is $50,000:

1% advertising budget	=	$500 per year	= $42 per month
3% advertising budget	=	$1,500 per year	= $125 per month
10% advertising budget	=	$5,000 per year	= $417 per month

Start-up expenses should include a budgeted amount for advertising. At least ten percent of the annual projected revenue should be the advertising/marketing budget for the first year that the business is operating. Generally, after those initial months, the studio will have received enough publicity that lower expenditures can be budgeted and spent in order to maintain the student base.

So how should this budgeted amount of money be distributed? The options are plentiful.

6.3 Print Advertisements

Print advertising is around us everywhere, from our clothes and shoes, to the Sunday newspaper sale advertisements. The trickiest question surrounding print advertisement is ascertaining where it will get the biggest "bang for your buck."

6.3.1 Display Advertisements

Newspaper display advertisements are a common form of print advertisement. These advertisements are very popular but can also be costly. Despite the fact that they are not always a frugal option, when well done, they can offer a highly successful return.

The first step in setting up a display advertisement is to determine the newspaper that will best suit the needs of the business. Read local papers and see which ones consistently align themselves with the arts. Those papers already have the best targeted readership for the studio. Contact that paper to investigate display advertisement prices. No two newspapers ever have the same rates.

Begin by finding out the exact size of their column inch. The column inch is specified by the size of the finished page. Is the paper a traditionally sized page, or is it a tabloid style? After discovering the cost of a column inch, ask which days have higher readership and check whether the quoted rates change daily. For example, some papers have higher column inch prices for Sunday editions.

While on the phone inquiring about print advertisement information, ask for an ad representative to be assigned to you. An ad representative is a person who will be your designated contact person and will field your calls and questions regarding the studio account. This person should offer to design an advertisement to any requested size specifications. Ad design is a service offered by the newspaper and the ad representative and there should be no charge for this. Always insist on seeing a prototype of the advertisement so that it can be proofread before print time. From the beginning of this business association, work to promote a healthy relationship with the ad representative. This person can determine ad placement as well as offer discounts and deals that he or she may not present to all clients. In other words, this is a person who can help you and your business.

Offer enough information about the business so the ad representative has a reasonable understanding of what is being promoted. If the studio has a good strong logo design, offer it to the ad representative so that it may be incorporated into the display ad design. It's good to use this logo in every advertisement to promote immediate recognition by the public. An example of this instant association is the Nike "Swoosh." When the public sees that logo, they immediately identify and name the brand.

However, remember that an ad representative may not totally understand the business and may not be representing it in a way with which you are comfortable. If this is the case, ask for another representative. Since this service is being paid for, make a decision to change the representative change. Keep in mind also that the occupation of the ad representative is selling advertisements. Make certain that you are not pushed into a contract, ad size, or number of runnings that later you may regret as being unnecessary or too costly.

If you feel more comfortable setting up the display advertisement yourself, then do it.

There are countless studies regarding the set up and reading of display advertisements. Create something that will catch the eye.

Some things to keep in mind when creating a display ad:

- If the advertisement is too small, it may not be worth the price. This would generally be anything smaller than a 2-inch by 5-inch ad.
- A smaller advertisement will stand out better if it has a bold border around it.
- The places on the page near the reader's hands (as they hold the paper) are prime locations. That is where the eye goes.
- A crowded or busy advertisement is confusing to the eye. White space is often as important as the print.
- Always include the phone number and address!

As far as number of runnings, it's generally considered more beneficial to run a larger number of small advertisements than to run a smaller number of large advertisements. The budget will also determine this number.

If the cost of display ads in mass marketed newspapers removes this possibility from the realm of studio advertising options, then begin exploring other means to present information in print. There are many alternate publications for display ads. Elementary schools will have newsletters that go to the homes of every child enrolled. An advertisement in this newsletter could be very affordable and hit directly at the targeted market. The local high school will also present advertising possibilities at nominal rates; the programs for the fall orchestra concert, the musical, or any and all sporting events should be investigated as viable display ad options. Explore also the programs of the local university, symphony, or community theatre guild. These organizations will gladly insert your advertisement in their programs for an often affordable price.

Practical Application

Scenario:

Ann Smith is in the process of opening her music studio. She has an excellent, centralized, downtown location and already has a great start planning her business. She has contacted the only local newspaper which runs a biweekly Arts section as a regular feature and has been assigned an ad representative. Her ad representative has been very helpful, but Ann gets the impression that he doesn't quite understand her business.

Ann has also contacted one more smaller newspaper in town. She has never seen a copy of this newspaper, but a listing for the publisher appeared in the Yellow Pages.

Look at the following advertisements and determine which you think is the best.

Example 1

This is the advertisement that the ad representative put together from the fax that Ann sent him. During their short conversation, Ann and the ad representative mostly discussed her advertising budget. This advertisement fits the advertising budget that she had planned. At this point, Ann didn't have time to deal with the advertisement. Since the fax contained more than enough information and since the ad representative does this every day, she thought that the result would be just fine. After the call, Ann waited for the next newspaper to arrive, and this is what she found printed.

What are your reactions to this advertisement?

Example 2

This is the advertisement from the smaller newspaper. Ann feels this advertisement will save her money because it is so inexpensive compared to the other newspaper. The advertising department for this newspaper didn't seem to have time to take her call.

What are your reactions to this advertisement?

Music Lessons
Flute
Oboe
Clarinet
Saxaphone
Bassoon
555-1234

Example 3

This advertisement went through several revisions. Ann began by designing a "mock-up" on her laptop with her word processing application and the clarinet clip art she uses on her stationery. Ann showed the mock-up to several of her colleagues and made improvements before she contacted the newspaper. She then faxed this advertisement to the ad representative and he revised it by changing the font and adding the music notes. Ann liked the music note idea, but the ad representative, who has no musical background, didn't realize that the eighth note clip art he used was backwards. After the advertisement was revised one last time, this was the result. This advertisement fits the budget that Ann has planned.

Anne Smith WOODWIND instruction

Offering private and individualized music instruction for all ages and abilities.

Flute, Oboe, Clarinet, Saxophone, & Bassoon

123 East Main Street across from the Post Office

♪♪♪ **888-555-1234** ♪♪♪

What are your reactions to this advertisement?

Your Turn

Design a display advertisement that is approximately business card size.

Call the local newspaper and find out the size of a column inch. Design an advertisement that is approximately ⅛ page using the dimensions of this newspaper.

6.3.2 Classified Advertisements

Running a classified ad in the newspaper can attract students for a much smaller financial investment than a display ad. A section in the classifieds exists for Instruction, Self-Help, Children's Programs, or other similar headings. Find a heading that suits your needs, and place your advertisement there.

Try to write an advertisement that is twenty words or less. Concise and to the point is a requirement. The goal of a classified, or any other advertisement, for that matter, is to make the reader want to call to find out more about what you do.

Practical Application

Get a copy of the classified section of a local newspaper.

Write a classified ad with twenty words or less that will produce interest in your business. Use the newspaper for advertising ideas and also to decide which heading would include your advertisement.

6.3.3 The Press Release

The easiest and least expensive form of print advertisement is a press release. It is simple because you write it on your own time with your own exact content. No time is taken to set up an interview and you will never be misquoted. It is the least expensive because it is free. Please note, however, that there are a small percentage of newspapers who will not print a press release unless your business has an advertising account with them.

It is a good business practice to send your press release to the same newspaper that printed your advertisement.

Approach every event at the studio as a newsworthy item. Write a press release to announce it. Make the lead sentence direct and interesting. Keep the sentences to 23 words or less. The first mention of your name should include first name, middle initial, and last name. All subsequent mentions of your name should only use your last name. Use simple sentences with the fewest number of words.

A standard news release contains one or three or more paragraphs, never only two. The release should include the "W's:"
- What is the name of the business?
- What is the event?
- When will the event take place?
- Who are you?
- What levels and what instruments do you teach?
- Where is the location of the studio?

In the press release or advertising information, be as specific as possible, making sure to list the kinds of instruction offered (*i.e.* jazz, pop, blues, praise and worship, *etc.*) listed along with the instrument(s) of instruction.

Include even more specific information about offerings such as whether adults or preschool students are taught. Also include if you teach improvisation, playing by ear, theory and composition, *etc.* A head shot or some sort of photograph of you performing or teaching should be included with the press release. Plan on not having this photo returned to you.

After the initial press release to announce the opening of the studio, keep press releases as a constant form of advertising for the business. If twins perform in one of your duet recitals, that can be the subject of a press release. Take a picture of them and send it to the local paper with additional information about the recital. Always look for an interesting angle and capitalize upon it. When pictures of students are used, a release must be signed by a parent or guardian. See Appendix B.

Press releases should be used to announce:
- changes in the business, such as hours, curriculum, and staff
- additions to studio equipment or technology
- accomplishments of students
- special events and performances
- classes or workshops you have attended and additional certifications received

The format of a press release should begin with the date and the statement: **"FOR IMMEDIATE RELEASE."** Use one side of 8.5 by 11-inch white paper. Margins of at least an inch should be on all sides. Copy should be double-spaced. Go long on facts and short on adjectives, trying to keep the release to one page in length.

After the press release is written, conclude with contact information including email address, as well as telephone, and fax numbers.

At this time it is a good idea to have someone else proofread the release. A paragraph that is written by you and proofread by you may not be as easy to understand as you thought. Have a proofreader make certain that information is distinct and needs no further explanation.

Once the release is written, fax it to local papers with a request for placement. Do not expect instant results, as it will be printed at the newspaper's discretion. It may also be edited and amended by the newspaper.

Amass a list of appropriate fax numbers for the studio fax machine or computer so that they can be accessed quickly and easily. This will help encourage you to write frequent press releases.

It is easy to feel bothered by writing a press release after an event. The general feeling is, "I'm glad the event is over, let's move on." *Ingrain press release writing into your overall teaching experience*. Add it to the timetable of any studio activities. Press release writing should serve as the closure to all studio events.

At the end of the month, make a mental assessment of the events of the month. Are any of them newsworthy? If so, write a press release.

The importance of keeping the studio name in the public eye cannot be stressed enough, and neither can the importance of free publicity.

Practical Application

Use the information that has been presented regarding press releases, and write a prototype press release for the opening of your music instruction business.

6.3.4 Personal Interview

Another form of publicity is a personal interview. Set up this interview with the local newspaper, and suggest that they come and take a picture of you and your facility. Present an interesting angle so they will think that you are newsworthy and deserving of an article or feature. However, as alluded to previously in this chapter, be cautious and thoughtful with responses to questions. It is very easy to be misquoted. Only portions and paraphrases of your quotes and responses are used in an article, so keep this in mind. Present your information first, and then allow the interviewer to ask follow-up questions regarding the information.

6.3.5 Write a Column

Consider the possibility of writing a regularly scheduled column for a local newspaper. Use a topic that is near and dear to you. Address subjects such as music education, local cultural events, arts awareness, *etc*. Your name and business name will appear at the end of the article as a reminder to the readership that the business exists.

If you cannot find anyone interested in printing a self-penned column, then write letters to the editor. Controversial topics will raise interest and awareness. Address the lack of music and music education in our schools, the inequity our society places on choosing sports heroes instead of daily heroes, the Mozart Effect and its assets to education, or any other timely and somewhat debatable topic. At the end of the letter, once again, list your name and business name. This is another type of free publicity.

6.4 Other Printed Materials

There are several other forms of print material that can and should be explored. These include flyers, brochures, business cards, and direct mail letters of introduction. Other print ad options which are more costly include billboards and road signs. And, don't forget the simplest and most essential form of print advertising, a listing in the yellow pages of the local phone book.

6.4.1 Media Kit

Put together a media kit or promotional package for the business. The media kit should include extraordinary examples of:

* studio brochure or flyer
* business cards
* résumé
* references
* letter of introduction/cover letter
* a head shot for press releases
* articles, pictures and information about your students and alumni
* demo tapes/CDs

This kit should be used to introduce yourself to local media in the hopes of sparking the interest of a reporter or editor who will follow up by doing a feature on your studio. Any feature article that is written will give great exposure to the public at no cost to you!

A media kit should also be used to introduce yourself and your business to area musicians, educators, schools, and universities. This presentation will offer colleagues the freedom to learn about the studio first-hand, and they will see that your abilities are backed by your credentials. In the event that you opt not to send all of the media kit items, have them available so that they may be produced at a moment's notice.

Investigate available software to make professional looking brochures and business cards. Design a brochure and business card that reflects you, your personality, and qualifications, as well as what you would want the public to remember about the business.

The brochure should include:
- your name/the studio's name
- studio logo
- address
- phone number/fax number
- studio offerings; just as with a press release, be sure to list anything unique and unusual
- attendance/cancellation policies
- pricing
- any other pertinent information; *i.e.* if gift certificates are available or if you are available to perform for weddings and parties

Printed brochures can be a costly expenditure if they are professionally generated. If the business is on a small scale, computer-generated brochures are the best option.

Shop around for reputable printing companies. Look for quality work at a reasonable price. The yellow pages will list many business printers. Remember to get the highest quality available, and the largest quantity realistic for the business. If there is a deal offered on brochures in which the price is drastically reduced for 1,000, yet the original order was for 500, it still may not be worth it to purchase 1,000 brochures at a reduced rate. Think about how long it will take to use 1,000 brochures and whether they will be dated and stale looking before the supply is depleted. Not to mention, brochure modifications will surely need to occur as the instruction prices increase. Odds are at least 250 of the brochures that were purchased at such a great price will be thrown away. It is a wiser investment to purchase the number needed at a higher price per brochure than a greater number at a lower price.

Business cards have less information and are less specific. Barring the chance that there will be a change of address or phone number in the near future, it is safer to go ahead and buy or print business cards in larger quantities.

> *Always have business cards with you.*

This is just a fact of life in the business world. While it is true that you are a musician and an educator, you must now think like a business person as well. No business man or woman is ever without their business card.

The media kit should also include your résumé (see Chapter 10 for specific information on résumés and résumé writing).

6.4.2 Direct Mail

Direct mailing can be a cost-effective way to advertise if the correct mailing groups have been identified. Mailing direct can be as simple as sending a postcard or a brochure, or as elaborate as sending a cover letter accompanied by a media kit.

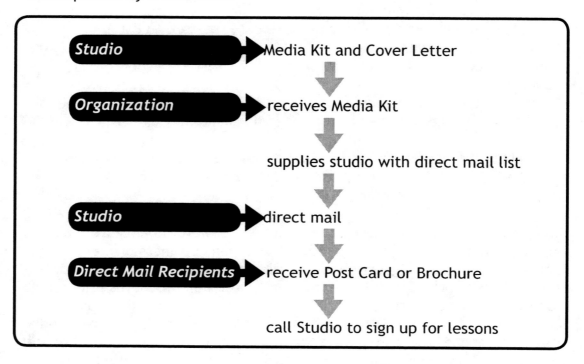

Media kit mailings should be made to locations that cater to the ages and interests of the students being sought. Mailing lists can be obtained from many different organizations. Demographic break-downs will offer this · information as well.

In an effort to network and get direct mail names, here are some possible locations to send media kits and introductory letters:
- local schools, both private and public
- universities
- churches
- theatre companies
- dance schools
- preschools
- Parent Teacher Associations/Organizations
- Cub Scouts/Girl Scouts
- YMCA
- Boys and Girls Clubs
- other "kid friendly" locations

Personalize the cover letter to the specific organization. Let them know:
- who you are
- what you offer
- why you will be so valuable to them

Use the following letters as guides to help in the authoring of your own direct mail instructional introduction cover letter.

Dear Fellow Educator,

The _____ Studio is a music instruction facility located in _____ which offers quality private music instruction in _____. Let me introduce myself. My name is _____ and I direct the _____ Studio. You will find more information about my experience and education by perusing the portfolio and media information that I have enclosed.

I offer weekly lessons in conjunction with a full curriculum to beginning, intermediate, and advanced musicians ages _____ through _____. School-age students are encouraged with incentive programs that reward practice and performance. Efforts to expand the offerings continually take the program in new directions.

Currently, I am seeking students and am asking for your assistance. Your school is highly regarded for the educational value it places on the arts. Would you consider sharing my name with your students? I would like to reach the families in your student body who might be most receptive to an educational opportunity of this nature. Could you possibly pass out flyers or allow me to send them to students who you feel might be interested or might benefit from private music instruction?

Please feel free to call _____ with any questions or to request more flyers. I would appreciate the opportunity to set up a meeting to discuss these educational offerings.

Thank you for your support.

Sincerely,
Your Name

Dear Fellow Educator,

The _____ Studio will once again be offering the [Your Music Education Program] in the Fall. This music education program is based upon the [your state] Academic Standards for Music as it implements an effective quality music curriculum for instrumental instruction. Offerings are on a 6-week or 9-week basis depending on the grading period already established by your school. This curriculum offers [name the school] students the opportunity for quality private music instruction while they are there in the comfort of their own learning environment. [If you are able to offer ensemble instruction as well, you could mention that here.] Please allow me the opportunity to present this information to your student body.

Educational research indicates that students involved in music do better in their academic pursuits. These students tend to be more creative, innovative, self-disciplined, and have considerably more advanced critical thinking skills. In addition, the College Entrance Examination Board has verified that students involved in music perform better on the SATs.

Through the [Your Music Education Program], private music lessons are offered to students on [list instruments you can teach]. Methods used include [traditional, improvisation, Suzuki, *etc.*]. Traditionally these lessons have been offered during the school day during lunch, study time, recess, music class or after school. Tuition rates vary according to the number of weeks involved in the instructional period.

I am interested in offering this service as an addition to the [name the school] curriculum. I would appreciate the opportunity to discuss these offerings with you. Please feel free to call _____ with any questions or if you would like more information. I have enclosed a media kit for your perusal.

Thank you for your time.

Sincerely,
Your Name

Include flyers that could be posted on the classroom bulletin board to attract new students. See Appendix C.

A cold mailing, meaning the information is being sent to a name that came off a list, will probably be the most economical if a postcard or brochure is sent. There is no need to spend the extra money on the printing and mailing of a cover letter and media kit. The post card or brochure will share all the information necessary with the prospective student.

When generating a direct mail postcard or flyer, look at what attracts your eye and design something with that in mind. Consider also including some sort of discount coupon in the direct mailing. See 6.6.1 for specific discount ideas.

If a flyer is desired, make certain that the increased expense of postage and printing over that of a post card is worthwhile and warranted. If everything can be said in a postcard-sized mailing, then use it instead.

Two hundred pieces of mail constitutes a bulk mail rate. Check and see what the cost is on a local bulk rate. Make sure it is worth the investment before making a financial commitment.

Once again, make sure someone else proofreads your materials. Remember, something that makes perfect sense to you can seem ambiguous and confusing to another reader.

Practical Application

Write a letter of introduction to a local school or organization. Include all the pertinent information about yourself and what you offer. List your pricing and also offer a price reduction for the first ten new students who respond to this appeal.

6.4.3 Road Signs

Road signs and billboards are advertising options that offer superb exposure to the general public. Although the market is not targeted as in direct mail or print ads placed in arts periodicals or programs, the results can still be resounding.

Everyone sees billboards. Look at the bottom of the billboard and get the name of the company who owns it. Look on the web or in the Yellow Pages for the company name and contact them. Let them know the location of the board you are interested in, as well as your type of business. (Sometimes, if they find out you're a small business, they will give you a reduced rate.) The price escalates in a direct relationship with the number of cars projected to drive past that location each week.

Billboards are often expensive. There will be a monthly rate as well as a set-up/design price to pay. Assess the scope of this business and the projected or actual amount of money to be spent. Although pricey, one month of the studio name and logo on a well-placed billboard may do more for the business than any other form of advertising. Another perk stems from the fact that a billboard takes little time and effort on your part. It gets a big "bang for the buck," without much effort.

A sign that is not a billboard can be built and kept in a permanent location. Rent or purchase the land on which the sign is placed. This may sound expensive, but, depending on location, this option is often a more reasonable price than a billboard.

Instructors can also look at signs as a great way to offer bartering of lessons. If there is a student or prospective student who lives on a prime piece of real estate, offer to barter lessons for the placement of a sign on their property.

Contact local sign makers and give them your design ideas. Ask them for an estimate. They will put together a design and quote a price. This price should include construction of the sign as well as installation. This company should know the rules of sign placement in the area, *i.e.* how far from the road, how large is permissible, *etc*. If they don't know the answers to these questions then you should probably find another sign maker or contact local government offices on your own to find the answers to your sign questions.

Insist on strong, readable designs. Black and white, red, and neons are the best eye-catchers. Signs do not need to be illuminated. Have the sign maker use reflective sign materials and the sign will shine back at the headlights of oncoming traffic at night. Depending on location, illumination may be an unnecessary expense.

6.4.4 Public Bulletin Boards

Place flyers, brochures, and business cards in busy public areas such as banks, libraries, parks, churches, and grocery stores. Some locations such as music stores, book stores, and laundromats may have a bulletin board area or will allow local advertisements in the window.

Consider making a pocket on the flyer to house studio business cards. This would be preferable to the less professional flyers that we have all seen that have the phone numbers that are ripped off the bottom of the sheet.

Once locations are established and flyers are placed, check them periodically. Sometimes flyers are inadvertently ripped down, or just look weathered and marred. Change the flyer content occasionally. Rather than having just a general content flyer, create one that addresses specific issues such as senior students, preschool students, jazz-improvisation instruction, or anything that is more specific than the usual flyer. Alternate studio flyers with specific flyers.

6.4.5 Yellow Pages

A basic and necessary advertising requirement is the phone book. This is the only advertising alternative presented in this chapter that is mandatory. The yellow pages are still used by most people as the first source consulted when looking for and deciding upon a service. Along with the listing in the white pages, it is well worth the financial investment to put a listing in the yellow pages.

If finances allow, classify in the yellow pages of all the phone books used in the area. If this is financially impossible, select the book that was delivered when the phone line was installed. Some phone companies will offer the option of including the yellow pages print price with the monthly phone bill. Research this option.

There are two possible headings under which the studio can be listed in the yellow pages. Some studios choose to print under both headings for better recognition. This will add to the price, but may be worth the expenditure. Heading options are Music Instruction-Instrumental and Music Instruction-Vocal.

6.5 Non-Print Options

Just as there are many print options, there are also countless options for marketing that do not include print. As presented in Section 6.2 of this chapter, *The Standard Periodical Directory* and *The Media Factbook* are thorough resources which should be consulted for listings of print and non-print media. After establishing the advertising budget, consider incorporating and combining several forms of marketing media.

6.5.1 Radio

Local radio advertising is especially effective in a small town. Do not disregard the station simply because you do not listen to them. Find out the commercial and production rates for a 30 second radio spot and consider running one.

The radio station will put together a promotional package in which they will guarantee to run your spot a specified number of times in a given period of time. Generally the price per running drops incrementally as the number of runnings increases.

Explore the show listings of the radio station. Do they sponsor a talk show that highlights local events? The studio is an arts business in the community and its presence is newsworthy. Send a media kit and ask to be interviewed for that show.

If a radio interview is granted, remember that the responses to the questions must always be audible and should not be short answer such as simply saying "yes" or "no." Always elaborate.

Practical Application

Write the script that will be used for a thirty-second radio spot to introduce your music business to consumers. Address pertinent information by answering the "W" questions: Who are you? What do you do? Where are you located? Present this information in an attention-grabbing format that can be crammed into 30 seconds. Don't forget to include the phone number and other contact information.

6.5.2 Cable Television

Cable television is another non-print marketing option that can offer bountiful results. If the local cable company is nationally affiliated, the advertising prices will be quite high. However, in the event that the station is locally owned and operated, a thirty-second commercial could definitely be an advertising option to consider.

A commercial can either be shot on location or put together in the studio. A spot that's shot on location will be a little more costly since more than one employee from the company will need to be present at the filming. The editing will occur later at the studio. A studio-generated spot will be a more economical option since fewer steps and people are involved.

To make a studio commercial, give the cable staff a series of photos that show you and your business in positive educational situations. The studio will crop, edit, and place the pictures on film in an appealing order.

While the photos are being shown, there will be a voiceover announcer conveying your studio information. You will probably be expected to write the voiceover copy, but probably not permitted to perform it. Submit a copy of the music you prefer be used in the background under the voice over.

The cable account representative will offer varying rates for the number of times the commercial is run. The rate you pay to run each spot will be determined by the number of channels, the number of viewers, and the times of day your commercial airs.

6.5.3 Website

In this day and age, almost every business has some sort of online presence. In fact, many consumers have come to expect that the businesses with whom they deal have a website. Luckily, the process of designing a website and getting it online has become easier over time and less expensive.

The process for getting your music studio online includes five basic steps which include a few financial considerations. While there may be different methods to accomplish these steps, all of them will be addressed in some way if you decide to build a website.

1. **Decide upon the content you wish to include in your site.**

   You need not reinvent the wheel when you complete this step. Your Media Kit is a great place to start. It should contain most, if not all, of the information you will want on your website.

2. **Design the website.**

   If you have done any web design in the past, you probably already know that a major time commitment is involved in designing an excellent site. If you have never designed a site before, it might be best to find someone to help you with this process. Professional web design can be very expensive so you may wish to enlist the help of friends or even students. This may be another opportunity to barter; you offer lessons for website design and maintenance.

   Before committing to a web designer, ask to see other sites they have designed. If you like one of their current sites, tell them which features you would like to have on your site and get an estimate for the expected time it will take them to design your site. Better yet, ask them if they will design a prototype "front page" and a single "supporting page." This way, if you do not like the design, not much time or money has been invested.

   You don't actually need to have your web address established online to see your prototype web pages. A designer can show you your site in a web browser from a computer (such as a laptop) from a CD they have burned, or in a variety of other ways before your site actually goes online. This way, you can spread out some of your initial web project costs.

3. Secure your domain name

Your domain name is the technical term for your web address (www.yourstudioname.com). Domain names must be registered online through a variety of domain name registration sites. A reputable and well-established domain name registration service is www.networksolutions.com. This site explains the process of registering your name online. There is an annual fee to maintain a domain name which is between $25 and $75 at the time of this writing.

4. Find a web host.

A web host is a person or company who owns the web server (computer) where your website exists and can be accessed by any Internet user. Your web designer will need to know the method (usually via a network connection involving a username and password) to connect to the web host's server and transfer your website files to their computer. A web host can also offer you email hosting services so your email address will match your website address (annsmith@annsmithstudio.com could be your email address, for example). Most web hosts bill monthly or quarterly for the services they provide.

You may be aware that some companies offer free website space on their servers which will usually force users to see advertisements of other companies when they visit your site. Also, some Internet Service Providers offer web space to their subscribers. However, in most cases, businesses are not allowed to use these "free" services and your site could get shut down.

Always read the terms and conditions carefully when signing up for any web service.

5. Maintain your site.

Don't forget this crucial last step! It is very important that the information on your site be current. Even if you don't change your content every week or even every month, make sure such things as your program offerings, staff list, and tuitions are accurate. There's nothing more frustrating to an avid web user than a stale, inaccurate website.

Your website can be an excellent advertisement and public relations tool for your studio. Use it in creative ways to communicate and highlight your studio's strengths, staff, and students. Consider these and other possibilities in utilizing your site:

- issue a press release when your website "goes live"
- include sound or video of you or your students on your site
- create an alumni section which highlights your performing or otherwise successful students
- link your website with the chamber of commerce, local churches, educational sites, and other appropriate links. If you link to a site, email the website administrator and ask them for a reciprocal link back to your site.
- register your site with major search engines
- ask your web host for statistics (or "stats") on the number and type of visitors to your site. This provides an online "demographic" report of your visitors. A small monthly fee is usually charged for stats.

6.5.4 Public Speaking

If the lecture and public speaking circuit seems attractive, look for opportunities to speak at meetings and forums. Use some of the same topics that would ignite a good column or editorial. For example, contact the local MOPs (Mothers Of Preschoolers) groups and ask to speak about the value of early childhood music education. Present the Mozart Effect and other contemporary studies regarding young children and music and spatial learning. You'll be introduced to the audience as the owner of the studio. At the end of the presentation, have brochures and business cards available to anyone who wishes to chat.

Venues for lectures about music, music education, and the independent music business include library boards, arts collaboratives, college classes, senior citizens groups, small business associations, and the local Chamber of Commerce, to name a few.

Contact high schools and ask to be a guest speaker to band, choir, and orchestra students. Talk about the importance of private lessons and music education. Pass out cover letters and brochures to any interested students. Ask also to be a guest presenter at Career Day seminars.

If the idea of public speaking is not attractive to you, then consider one-on-one presentations. Write and memorize a 20-second elevator speech. Pinpoint your business in a short *"spiel"* that includes the business name and mission. Write it up and share it with colleagues. Does it make sense? Do the words and the delivery present the passion you have for your job?

6.5.5 Parades

Another interesting advertising option is to place a float in a local parade. This is a great opportunity to position the name of the business in front of the eyes of an audience of thousands of people who will give you their undivided attention. Ask friends and family to help construct the float or enlist the assistance of students. This is a chance for students to build a bond with other private music students and a loyalty and pride in the studio. Those same students who help with construction could ride and perform on the float or distribute flyers that tell the basics of the studio along the parade route. If the studio is a new business and there are no students to pass out flyers, offer a donation to the 4-H club or a church youth group of your choice and in return their members will walk the parade route and pass out the studio flyers.

Entry fees for parades are minimal. The expense for this form of advertising comes from the supplies purchased to build the float.

6.5.6 Performances

Acquaint the general public with the name of the studio, your students, and yourself by participating in community performances. Performances allow students to bring the gift of music to others while bringing the gift of advertising to the studio. See Chapter 8 for information and listings of location options for community performances.

6.6 Alternate Promotional Activities

There are still more promotional advertising activities that are not associated with commercial media of any kind. Explore the possibilities of using one of the following.

6.6.1 Open House or Grand Opening

Contemplate sponsoring an open house. This promotion is especially good when opening a store-front music business. Send invitations to arts and educationally-friendly organizations as well as the local media. Hang banners and signs and open the door to the public. Grand Openings should offer:

- **giveaways, such as one month of free lessons**
  This is a terrific idea since, once a student begins instruction, odds are they'll get hooked on lessons and continue studying and (more importantly) paying for a much longer time than the one month that was free.

- **free t-shirts**
  Everyone gets excited about a free t-shirt. Design something or have a screen printer develop a design. Have a drawing, and give the shirts away.

- **music-related items**
  Look in music merchandise catalogs to find inexpensive products such as cups, water bottles, mugs, and pens. Use these items for door prizes and raffles.

- **food**
  Be creative. Custom cookie shapes or a musically-themed cake are inexpensive and tasty options.

Expect to be contacted by the Chamber of Commerce and asked to join. Depending on the size and activity of the chamber, joining may be a viable and beneficial option and well worth the annual membership fee. A Chamber of Commerce should be able to offer help with the execution of a grand opening or open house. The Chamber will advertise the open house as well as announce it to other businesses in the organization. A Chamber officer may attend the opening and perform a ribbon cutting ceremony. This, of course, is a very newsworthy activity in small town America. Request a photographer and have a media kit ready for any press person who attends.

6.6.2 Sponsor an Activity

Sports teams are always seeking sponsors and boosters. Information regarding sponsorship can be obtained from the league director or board of directors. Investigate the feasibility of the studio sponsoring a team. This option will present the studio name and logo on t-shirts that will be worn by team members and placed before spectators for an entire season. These types of sponsorships are often very affordable.

Just as the major sporting events offer and require sponsorship, so do smaller, local sporting events such as a 5K race, a tennis tournament, or a cheerleading camp. These events also may offer t-shirts to participants who will in turn wear the studio name and logo for the entire next year.

Other sponsorships are also available. If there is a student from the studio who is competing in a contest or pageant, their participation in this event is an indirect advertisement for the studio. It is a thoughtful and supportive gesture to sponsor that student.

6.6.3 Good Will Kits

Studio materials can be distributed as part of good will kits at hospitals to new parents and through realtors to new residents.

The Welcome Wagon is a national organization which gives promotional packets to new members of a community. Those packets could include promotional and discount offers along with an introduction to the studio and its services. A pen or business card magnet would serve as a studio reminder to the new resident.

New parents are given many complimentary items as they exit the hospital with their newborn. Even if the studio does not offer programs to young children, it is a wise marketing move, as well as educationally sound, to introduce parents to studio offerings. Offer promotional materials and discount offers accompanied by cute musical rattles (purchased at the dollar store) or bibs with studio logo imprinted on them. Include an introductory letter that states, "The time to start thinking about your child's musical education is at birth." Follow that lead-in with information about the studio and music instruction. After all, the newborn may also have older siblings.

6.6.4 Giveaways and Discounts

The American public is always attracted to a bargain. Use a special offer to entice students into the front door. Propose whatever discount the budget will permit. Remember, once students have experienced the studio and private instruction, most will continue the lessons after the expiration of the promotion. Some proposed discounts include:

- two-for-one discounts
- new student discounts
- family discounts
- day-time lesson discounts
- late-night lesson discounts
- home-school student discounts
- senior citizen discounts
- referral discounts
- free trial lesson

Offer any one of these reductions, keeping in mind that the promotion can easily be a limited-time offer. When advertising these discounts, remember to include the benefits as well as the features. For example, due to limited lesson time slots available, the first ten new students who sign up as a result of this campaign will receive a 20% discount for the first three months. This should serve as an incentive to entice new students. Always use comments such as, "This will save you $100." The public responds very well to obvious financial savings. Discount incentives also ask prospective students to take immediate action and provide a motivation for them to do so.

6.6.5 Raffles

Raffles are also a popular American phenomenon. When hosting a raffle, ask for specific information on the sign-up sheet. This sheet can then be used to formulate a mailing list of possible future music students. These people should be sent a brochure and studio information.

Music Studio Raffle

Name _____

Address _____

Phone _____

Instrument of Interest _____

Age of Student _____

The prize could be one to three months of free lessons for themselves or a gift certificate for a friend or relative. Depending on studio and instructor availability, more than one raffle winner can be selected.

Some of the possible activities where a raffle could be held include:
- arts-friendly festivals or fairs
- auctions where proceeds go to worthy causes
- philanthropic organization fundraisers
- PTA, PTO, or other school fairs and activities

Your name and the name of the studio will be publicly thanked for supporting this endeavor. You benefit from both the visibility of helping a good cause and from the mailing list of interested prospective students which came from the raffle box.

6.7 Additional Resources

If you wish to further study the concept of advertising and publicity for your music studio, please refer to the following comprehensive marketing resources:

- *Getting Publicity* (third edition) by Tana Fletcher and Julie Rockler, Self Counsel Press, 1704 N. State St., Bellingham, WA 98225 www.self-counsel.com
- *Marketing your Home-Based Business* by Jeffrey P. Davidson and Bob Adams, Inc., 260 Center St., Holbrook, MA 02343
- *High-Impact Marketing on a Low-Impact Budget: 101 Strategies to Turbo-Charge Your Business Today!* by John Kremer and J. Daniel McComas

6.8 Advertising Evaluation

One or several of the advertising options listed in this chapter will prove successful to you and your business. It may, however, take several attempts before finding the methods that bring in the most students. Each city and community is different. What works for one studio may not work for yours. It is imperative that you constantly and consistently evaluate and reevaluate your marketing efforts.

Steps to marketing analysis:
1. Avoid a single approach to marketing.
2. The goal of advertising is to attract the greatest number of customers. The most successful option may not be the one you like most. Be flexible enough to admit that.
3. Use varied methods of advertising according to the budget allocation.
4. Keep detailed, meticulous records that measure
   - time invested
   - cost of supplies
   - cost of phone/fax/gasoline
   - cost of actual advertising
5. Ask each person who inquires, "How did you hear about the studio?" Even if that person doesn't sign up for lessons, you need to know how they learned about you. This is the only way to find how your marketing is working.
6. After several months of varied marketing efforts, evaluate the phone responses to determine the most successful options.

After you have gathered some data:
- Identify what has been the most effective advertising during this time period.
- Evaluate the return versus the time and money invested.
- Constantly evaluate and contemplate improvements.
- Don't be afraid to experiment.

6.9 Summary

In order for your business to receive a successful response from the public, some form of advertising will be required. Since the budget for many teachers is limited, it is important to target the market.

The initial advertising expense will likely be higher than the projected monthly budget. With success the studio will eventually be fueled by word of mouth recommendations.

Many options are available for the advertising dollar. Consider print advertisements first. These can take the form of newspaper display ads, and though costly, they can offer a highly successful return. Decide on a publication which will reach the targeted market and compose a concise advertisement that is eye-catching as it gives pertinent information. Running a classified ad can attract students for a much smaller financial investment than a display ad. Place the advertisement under a suitable heading.

A well-written press release is a valuable tool and will likely be free, especially if you use the same newspaper where a print or classified ad was placed. Press releases can be used on numerous occasions and should be a built-in part of your overall teaching experience.

Make yourself available for a personal interview with the local newspaper. Write a regular arts or music education column. Do not overlook flyers, brochures, business cards, and direct mail advertising.

A media kit or brochure about the business is beneficial. These should be distributed to locations such as schools and organizations that cater to the ages and interests of students being sought.

Road signs and billboards offer superb exposure to the general public. They can be pricey, but you will get a big "bang for the buck" without much effort.

Flyers, brochures and business cards can be posted or placed in public places for additional exposure. However, a basic and most necessary advertisement requirement is the yellow pages of the telephone book.

There are also non-print options available such as local radio ads. These advertisements can be written, read, and performed by you or your students.

In this computer-driven age, a website containing information from the media kit would be a valuable tool for reaching the public. Follow proper procedures by securing a domain name, choosing a web host, and maintaining your site by making sure everything is current at all times.

If public speaking is attractive to you, look for such opportunities with local organizations. Other alternate promotional activities could include an open house, grand opening, discounts, free promotions, activity sponsorship, goodwill kits, and raffles. It may take some time to find the best advertising plan for you, but be prepared to experiment, evaluating the effectiveness of each approach.

Practical Application

Allow yourself a monthly budget of 10% of your projected annual income (after taxes).

Research the local market and put together an advertising package that uses at least three different forms presented in this chapter. Include a financial breakdown of each marketing style selected.

CHAPTER 7

Maintaining Student Interest

7.1 Maintaining Student Interest

The predominance of reward orientation in today's society is apparent everywhere. Who hasn't seen the triumphant athlete holding the trophy, and shouting, "I'm going to Disneyworld!" In the mind of a child participant, an entire soccer season may be for naught if a trophy isn't earned. Whatever happened to performance for intrinsic value? Does there always have to be a reward? Can't the fact that a skill has been learned serve as reward enough? Unfortunately, the answers to these questions may be rather disappointing.

If you are vehemently opposed to reward systems and find them educationally compromising, unjust or invalid, then be warned that this chapter will annoy you. Perhaps skipping to the next chapter would be in your best interest. However, if a prize chest and candy jar sit on the bookcase right next to the metronome, then read on.

A recent survey of classroom teachers in Miami-Dade County Florida, states that 43% of all surveyed spend out-of-pocket amounts of $500 or more annually. A substantial portion of this amount is spent on incentives for the students. Twenty-nine percent stated that they spend from $300 to $400 annually. Incentive expenses are an understood part of instructional costs. Offering incentives will require a financial investment; nevertheless, the dollars spent may produce positive results in the motivation of many a reward-oriented elementary or middle school student.

7.2 Additions to the Curriculum

In today's society where the average eight-year-old is participating in soccer, baseball, scouting, skating lessons, dance, gymnastics, and church activities (to name just a few), private music lessons may have a tough time competing. Therefore, in order to vie with the myriad of activities offered to today's students, consider some of the curriculum-boosting ideas presented in this chapter. Extra options and additions to the curriculum may serve to extend student interest in this world of instant gratification, over-extenders, and over-achievers. One of these ideas may offer the added enticement to keep a student involved long enough to realize that music speaks to them in a way that other activities cannot.

7.2.1 Practice Incentives and Rewards

Keeping in mind that bribery (an incentive system) is one possible element of a music instruction curriculum, establish a prize area, box, or treasure chest. Purchase items the students will enjoy. Keep an eye on the current trends and don't forget to shop the dollar stores to pick up items that are both fun and inexpensive. Items or gift certificates that are educational or music-related are always appreciated by students and parents alike. Food gift certificates for McDonald's and Burger King, for example, are also enjoyed by the students.

Catalogs that offer appropriate music merchandise include:
- Music Treasures Company
- Music in Motion
- Music Stand
- Oriental Trading Company

These companies offer information both online and in mail order catalogs which can be sent to your home.

Personalized studio items can prove a viable consideration as award/reward options. Investigate printing costs for t-shirts, book bags, folders, and music bags. For example, use the studio logo design or a fun and whimsical music design and have it printed on a plain canvas bag or t-shirt. These items will be worn and carried with pride and ultimately can provide advertising for the studio. These items will cost more than dollar store finds, but should prove cost effective because of the dual functionality of incentive and advertising.

Let students know that prizes are not awarded randomly. Establish the award system, and stick to it.

When determining the award system:

1. Place age parameters on the students who will be eligible for the incentives.
2. Decide the possibilities for student rewards. Some workable options to consider may include:
   - a stellar lesson
   - a public performance
   - successful completion of a method book
   - attendance at a classical concert followed by a written review
   - completed levels of a music instructional computer program
   - a birthday
   - outstanding work or research (in a "composer of the month" program or "term of the month" program)
   - a weekly drawing or lottery from a pool of students who have achieved successful practice

Practical Application

You have a $100 budget. Using catalogs and online companies, make selections for incentive items for the opening of your studio. Include gift certificates as well as gift items. Include the following information:
- Company name
- Item name and order number
- Page number or Internet address
- Amounts and total

7.2.2 Student of the Month

Everyone loves a free t-shirt. Award a t-shirt or book bag to a student of the month. Have students place their name in a drawing box and pull the winning name. To determine the students who can place their names in the drawing, use some of the incentive criteria listed in Section 7.1.1 as well as:
- improvement
- practice consistency
- perseverance in difficult practice situations (such as a broken appendage or illness)
- musical accomplishments

7.2.3 Term and/or Composer of the Month

Acquaint students with classic and contemporary composers. This concept can be an exciting and interesting addition to the curriculum. Consider introducing a "composer of the month." Offer students composer information through:

Composer Information Sources

- website scavenger hunts ....www.eslpartyland.com (ESL Treasure Hunt on Music), www.bandsontheweb.com
- puzzles
- worksheets
- books ....*Meet the Great Composers*, by Montgomery and Hinso, *Classic Tunes and Tales*, by Kline *Great Composers of the 20th Century*, by Gibbons *Marsalis on Music*, by Marsalis
- videos ....:..............*Beethoven Lives Upstairs, Hallelujah Handel, Mr. Bach Comes to Call, Mozart's Magic Fantasy, Mozart's Magnificent Voyage, Tchaikovsky Discovers America, Vivaldi's Ring of Mystery, Handel's Last Chance, Bach's Fight for Freedom, Bizet's Dream, Rossini's Ghost*
- interactive software ....*Beethoven Lives Upstairs, Pianomouse Meets the Great Composers*

Students could complete one or several activities, write a report, or design a poster using their discoveries. As an extension of composer appreciation activities, assign students original or arranged repertoire by the composer to coincide with research and activities.

Composer selection could be either random or in conjunction with their own birthday. Appendix D offers a birthday list of some of the major composers.

Another possible curriculum addition introduces the "term of the month." Present and review terms of the month to students of all levels. Offer musical words, names, phrases, and expressions. Students can take responsibility for finding and writing the definitions. Assign repertoire that contains or demonstrates each term. This addition is an excellent opportunity for reinforcing a concept or term so that it is learned, retained, and ultimately mastered.

If the rigors of preparation associated with selecting and maintaining these curriculum additions become too consuming, consider having a composer or term only two or three times per year rather than monthly. This may serve to assure that the activity is viewed as an exciting endeavor rather than a tedious exercise.

Some students who require extra encouragement may need to be awarded studio incentives for their investigative work into the composer or term of the month. However, students will not likely see a need for rewards if the composer or term of the month activities are required from the onset of lessons. This will be viewed as a usual part of the instructional curriculum.

Practical Application

1. Select a sample composer to be highlighted in your teaching.
2. Select a sample term to be highlighted in your teaching.
   - Find two websites that will provide the students with information about the composer.
   - Design a game or puzzle about the composer.
   - Design a game or puzzle the utilizes the term of the month.
   - Find two pieces of representative literature that offer a beginning or early intermediate student a glimpse at the composer.
   - Find two pieces of representative literature (for your instrument) that demonstrate the term of the month.

7.2.4 Awards

To trophy, or not to trophy...that is the question.

If the studio clientele consists primarily of students who are high school age and younger, then using trophies as incentives may be a consideration. Trophies may be additions to the curriculum that will prove well worth their financial investment. The fact that the studio offers trophies can somehow make it more viable in the eyes and egos of students. Trophies can be purchased for minimal cost and provide maximum student interest and response.

Specific questions regarding the awarding of trophies include:
- Will practice be rewarded?
- Will award recipients be determined solely by the instructor, or by a combination of evaluation by the student, others, and the instructor?
- Will awards be distributed by use of a point system? If so, what will the point system be?
- Will awards be distributed to students for improvement?
- Will awards be distributed to students for outstanding work, discipline or performance?
- Will awards (trophy size) increase in parallel increments to the studio point reward system?
- Will awards be annual?
- Will trophies, certificates, pins, or ribbons be awarded?

Investigate trophy companies for competitive prices and shipping rates.
- Crown Awards   www.crownawards.com
- Dinn Brothers Trophy   www.dinntrophy.com
- Trophy Depot   www.trophydepot.com

If trophies are not in the budget, the use of pins, ribbons, and certificates for reward purposes are less expensive options. The trophy companies listed above will be sources for other reward items as well. Design or discuss with the studio printer the creation of a certificate of merit using the business logo. The use of parallel designs for brochures, business cards, the website, and certificates presents a thoughtful and professional package. See Appendix E for a sample studio brochure.

Practical Application

Determine a point system for studio awards. Put it in a package format that can be presented to students at the time of their enrollment in the case statement.

List:
1. Five standards for which points will be awarded.
2. Point values assigned to each of these standards.
3. The number of points it takes to earn:
   - certificates
   - pins
   - ribbons
   - trophies

7.3 Special Events

Special events help rekindle the interest of both students and instructors. Seek special events that can stimulate the student without adding a great deal of expense to the studio and instructor. These are the events that may serve to keep young musicians working and practicing during challenging times such as summer, winter vacation, or spring break.

7.3.1 Summer and Holiday Activities

School age students often have difficulty adhering to their practice routines during holiday and vacation periods; this is a time when family schedules tend to change and priorities alter. The industrious private music instructor must apply added effort in order to pique interest and improve musicianship. After all, this is a business and a livelihood and it must be maintained even during the holidays.

For the winter break period, offer added practice incentives for students who attempt to or succeed at successful work and practice over the holiday. Some possible holiday options include:
- double the usual practice rewards
- lessen the practice time that is typically required
- take a field trip
- have a holiday party

Summer is an excellent time to improve technique and general skill levels. Many families remove their children from lessons for the summer. Discourage this by pointing out how much progress can be made during this time. There are seldom any contests or recitals scheduled during summer months; this performance void allows the focus of instruction to be placed solely on the advancement of skills. Summer offers an opportunity to diverge from the ordinary and make extraordinary improvements. This is a vital point which must be convincingly presented and stressed to all students.

The concentration of intense skill-building should be balanced with interesting and unusual activities and additions to the curriculum:
- Schedule a master class. Invite a colleague or former student to come and perform and/or to critique student performances.
- Pursue group instruction (especially if it isn't offered during the school-year).
- Offer buddy or group lessons in addition to regularly scheduled private instruction.
- Plan a field trip to a music exhibit, community music performance, instrument factory, or any other location that may have musical, educational, and entertainment value.
- Call the local university and ask if they have student recitals scheduled during the summer months. Take a field trip that will inspire and entertain.
- Encourage students to attend a summer music or other arts camp.
- Sponsor contests utilizing studio technology or Internet music site scavenger hunts.
- Award prizes for the overall high scores on computer music games.
- Plan a Summer Music Olympics. Work at making this a highly regarded and looked-forward-to activity. Place the students into teams and announce an afternoon of music-related relays, games, contests and activities. End the afternoon with treats, awards, and perhaps an impromptu jam session.

Any one of these activities and additions could keep the interest of a student who may plan to quit for the summer.

7.3.2 Community Performances

There are many options for recital-like performances for private music students. These opportunities consist of community performing occasions which serve as excellent venues for student performance while simultaneously providing studio publicity and exposure.

During the month of May, many communities recognize and celebrate the importance of the arts in conjunction with Music in Our Schools Month. Look for events that feature young musicians in performances at malls, churches, synagogues, book stores, art exhibits, and schools. If your community currently does not recognize or support Music in Our Schools, perhaps this could be an opportunity for your studio to organize music appreciation performances that highlight the talents of local student musicians (spearheaded by you and your studio and featuring your students, of course).

Year-round student performing opportunities to investigate include:
- book stores such as Barnes and Noble or Borders which often sponsor student musical performances
- nursing homes, hospitals, and senior centers seek entertainment for their residents and guests
- monthly meeting of the Chamber of Commerce, VFW, Rotary or similar club or organization
- holiday parties for businesses, religious groups, philanthropic, or community organizations

An option especially for pianists or string students comes from local dance companies who voice interest in live accompaniment for a dance recital or advanced class. This is also an opportunity for advanced students to make a little extra cash as these gigs should pay (and pay well!).

Weddings are an opportunity to showcase talent. If your studio earns a reputation for having quality wedding performers, the possibilities are limitless. If this is a direction that you believe you would like to take your studio or yourself, it will be worth the advertising investment. Put ads in classifieds or rent a booth at a bridal fair. Weddings pay well for the limited time investment and the limited amount of repertoire that needs to be mastered.

Contact local elementary and middle schools and introduce an end-of-the-year music workshop. These workshops or performances, offered to traditional or music classrooms by you and/or your students, are another example of positive press. When the classroom instructor is packing up the room and looking for things to do to keep students occupied, they will be receptive to activities that offer a diversion from the ordinary. Present a small performance or class that includes yourself and any students available. At the end of the performance or workshop tell the children what your studio has to offer during the summer. Make the presentation entertaining and FUN!

All of the presentation opportunities that showcase you and/or your students serve a dual purpose as they strengthen student performance skills and supply indirect studio advertising.

Studio recitals are an expectation associated with private music instruction. See Chapter 8 of this text is devoted to recitals.

7.3.3 Contests and Festivals

Sponsor an in-studio contest that will stretch the students and supply a little healthy competition as well. Devise a catchy title, "B#" for example. Include puzzles, worksheets, activities, and research topics that will require students to display knowledge that has been learned in your curriculum. Divide students into age and ability appropriate groups or teams, assign a length of time in which the contest must be completed, and let the students get to work.

Sponsor an in-studio performance festival or contest. A festival or contest promotes study, stimulates interest in quality musical literature, and encourages each participant to reach a high standard of musical achievement. This is especially exciting to a student who has never been a part of this kind of activity or had to perfect a selection to the degree required and expected by an adjudication situation. Of course, there are high expectations in weekly lessons and in recital performances, but a festival or contest, with critique, comments, or adjudication is an opportunity for a student to perfect their musical skills and performance abilities.

Students learn the fine points of preparation, technique, and performing by preparing a piece for evaluation either in competition or festival setting.

Determine and publicize:
- date and location of event
- student eligibility
- fees and costs
- applications

Make decisions regarding entry categories *i.e.* solo, sight-reading, duet, improvisation, and other performance requirements:

- with music or memorized
- with or without an audience
- one or multiple pieces
- required or choice selections

Make decisions regarding performance levels and divisions by ability levels ratings and how they will be assigned. Decide how results will be recognized *i.e.* certificates, ribbons, trophies, *etc.*

All festival information should be addressed in a student packet or mailing which includes the application, permission letter, and all other pertinent information. See Appendix F for a sample festival sign-up sheet.

Hire friends and colleagues to adjudicate or critique. Don't forget to write "thank you" notes to all who have helped, even those who have been offered a stipend.

Contests and Festivals Pros and Cons

Pros of a festival or contest:
1. Students must master a piece.
2. Comments that have been made during instruction will be echoed by the adjudicator.
3. Opportunity for study of broader repertoire.
4. Parents see the accomplishment and educational value.
5. Students have the opportunity to hear and see others perform.

Cons of a festival or contest:
1. A high level of organization is required.
2. Planning time will offer no financial remuneration.
3. Some students and parents are opposed to any "competition" in music.

7.3.4 Area and Nationally Sponsored Contests and Festivals

Consider becoming a member of a professional teaching organization. These associations offer opportunities to enhance the offerings of the independent music instructor. They sponsor contests, festivals, clinics, workshops, as well as publish journals and reviews of new repertoire. Through membership in these organizations you will have the opportunity to be a part of a national or international organization.

Some possible options to investigate include:
- [Your] State School Music Association
- National Guild of Piano Teachers
- National Federation of Music Clubs
- National Association of Teachers of Singing
- American String Teacher Association
- Music Teachers National Association

7.3.5 Journaling

Older students can establish their goals for music instruction in a written format. Require them to keep a journal in order to see when and if their goals are met. Set up a one-on-one in which you and the student spend time together out of the lesson environment.

7.3.6 Parties and Activities

Build a sense of camaraderie between studio students.

Host a studio party. Look for fun and interesting topics and allow students to gather and bond over and through their studio experiences.

Adults:

Host/sponsor a wine and cheese party which features student performances. A party is a great opportunity for normally introverted adult music students to perform for their peers. Strive to establish a comfortable and inviting performance environment and encourage discussion—not critique—among the students.

Host an open mic or karaoke night. Make a coffee house atmosphere that encourages all types of performances.

Adults and Teens:

Sponsor a "bad music party." Invite students to bring CD's, recordings, and videos to share that are what they consider "bad music." Ask them to critique the performances and make general observations regarding them.

(*Attention vocalists*: if you've never heard the Florence Foster Jenkins CD, now's the time to buy it!) Use this evening as an opportunity for students to bond and to talk about what makes quality music.

Elementary and Middle School Students:

Sponsor a theme party and ask students to perform for each other. Play games and do theme-related activities.

For example:
- piano pizza party (talk about Italian composers)
- Sponge Bob Square Pants party (introduce Water Music)
- Disney costume party (play Disney songs)

7.4 Elements of Music Games and Activities

There are numerous resources which present games and activities that will teach the elements of music. Books, workbooks, websites, and computer software can all be accessed to teach the elements of music. See Appendix G for some game ideas.

7.5 Newsletter

Send a newsletter home to parents seasonally, monthly, or weekly. Use this correspondence as an opportunity to present scheduling changes, financial reminders, progress reports, and news about yourself and your students. Announce area cultural happenings and events which may be of interest to students and their families.

Present the newsletter on paper, via email, or both. This will provide assurance that an adult has seen information from at least one medium.

7.6 Repertoire Class

Consider expanding the basic curriculum by adding a group class, ensemble, or buddy lessons to private studies. Many studios offer and/or require group lessons as part of their offerings to private students.

The time that would have been spent in private instruction during the ensemble instruction week is considerably less since several group lessons are taught instead of multiple private lessons. There will be a different preparation involved for a monthly group lesson.

7.6.1 Additional Classes

Offer a theory, music history, or technology class in addition to private instruction. A class of this nature, even for three or four students, can be very beneficial. If time and interest permit, consider these offerings to supplement the existing private curriculum.

Investigate to determine if students can receive high school credit for music classes offered at your studio. Depending on state standards and requirements, studio classes in theory, appreciation, or even applied studies may allow the students to receive credits from their school. This would entail the establishment of a specific curriculum, text, and student evaluations, but once again, this may be an educationally or financially positive addition to the studio curriculum.

7.7 Children's Programs

Would it benefit the studio to add a children's music program to the studio curriculum? There are a myriad of programs for infants and preschoolers which are readily available to educators. These programs can be implemented for minimal cost and training, as they require instructional seminars (one to five days in length) which present lesson plans and teaching strategies in their methodology. Decide if these existing class programs are feasible.

Some possibilities include:
- *Kindermusik*   www.kindermusic.com
- The Children's Garden   www.childrensgardenstudio.com/music.html
- Musicgarten   www.musikgarten.org
- Music Together   www.musictogether.com
- Harmony Road Music   www.harmonyroadmusic.com
- Music for Young Children www.myc.com

Practical Application

Upon reviewing all the ideas presented in this chapter, select five that ideas to maintain student interest that best reflect your personality. List specific reasons for their selection.

7.8 Summary

An incentive system is a justifiable element of a music instruction curriculum. Establish a prize area, box, or treasure chest, and purchase items for it that the students will enjoy. Establish an award system which places age parameters and specific guidelines for students to be awarded a prize. Look for ways to embellish the curriculum itself by introducing a composer or term of the month. Trophies are one of those additions to the curriculum that will prove well worth the financial investment. If trophies are not in the budget, the use of pins, ribbons, and certificates for reward purposes are less expensive options.

Special events help rekindle the interest of the student and the instructor as well. These are the events that may serve to keep young musicians working and practicing during challenging times such as summer, winter vacation, or spring break.

Schedule a masters class, pursue group instruction, plan a field trip to a music exhibit, community music performance, instrument factory, or any other location that may have musical, educational, and entertainment value.

Sponsor contests utilizing studio technology or internet music site scavenger hunts. Or, give prizes for the overall high scores on computer music games. Plan The Summer Music Olympics.

There are many options for recital-like outside performances for private music students. Look for events that feature young musicians in performances at malls, churches, synagogues, book stores, art exhibits, holiday parties, club meetings and school activities. Contests and festivals are also a good way to alter the usual schedule. Sponsor an in-studio contest that will stretch the students and supply a little healthy competition as well. An in-studio performance festival or contest is a great curriculum additive. Enter students in an area nationally sponsored contest or festival as well.

Investigate was of expanding the basic curriculum by adding class instruction in history, theory, or applied music. Or, by adding a children's music instruction program.

CHAPTER 8
Recitals

8.1 Recitals

As directed by the case statement guidelines, programs and services offered by the studio should be disclosed to prospective students and their families. Recitals are an expected aspect of private music instruction and should be included in the case statement.

One of the primary goals of private instruction is to teach the art of performance. Recitals present a receptive and friendly performing environment. Unfortunately just the mention of a recital strikes fear into the hearts of young and old, beginning and seasoned performers alike. A recital is also a major time and money commitment for the studio and instructor; however, a recital is always worth the effort.

Students reap countless benefits from preparing and ultimately presenting a piece to an audience. Students and parents alike should be reminded that the ability to survive and perform in front of a crowd nurtures the kind of poise that is required in countless vocations.

Besides, a recital is possibly some of the best publicity available. A room full of friends, family, and neighbors can spread the wonders of your studio instruction by word of mouth faster than any print ad or press release available.

Many studios charge a recital fee to help defray the cost of a facility and the hiring of a sound technician. A $20 per participant fee seems to be the average. If this will be the case, then present this information at the time of enrollment.

8.2 Student Preparation

There are many other aspects involved in preparing a student for performance, and these must be addressed by the private music instructor.

8.2.1 Performance Preparation

Tape record or videotape each student's rehearsal program. Analyze and evaluate the rehearsal tape before the actual performance.

Pianists should play/practice their recital piece on as many different pianos as possible before the recital performance.

Girls should bow, not curtsy. All should bow to acknowledge applause. Stress to students that applause is a gift, and not bowing is the same as not saying "thank you," for a gift. Tell them to always keep their feet together throughout a bow. Always bow your head and don't try to keep eye contact with the audience. This is something that will need to be rehearsed, especially with younger students.

Always acknowledge the accompanist. This too will need to be taught to the students. Also, practice in performance clothes and shoes. Remind students that it's important to think through the piece 5 times and play it only once. This will help with performance anxiety and memorization problems.

8.2.2 Performance Anxiety

Talk with students about all the aspects of the performance. This includes performance anxiety.

Performance anxiety may manifest itself either before, during, or after a performance. The first step to lessen anxiety is to identify and accept nervousness as a commonplace and normal part of performance and performance preparation. These manifestations can be:
- physical manifestations such as rapid heart beat, sweaty or cold hands
- cognitive manifestations such as worry or mental block
- behavioral manifestations such as the inability to prepare or practice appropriately due to avoidance performance anxiety

The Private Music Instruction Manual: A Guide for the Independent Music Educator • Rebecca Osborn

Use this assessment to examine feelings about performing with both inexperienced as well as more seasoned performers. As with all problems, just recognizing and labeling them will help. A healthy attitude towards performance is a skill which can be learned.

Performance Anxiety Inventory

Circle your response to each scenario.

Before performance,
I feel nauseated.................. Almost Never   Sometimes   Often   Almost Always

During performance,
my hands sweat .... Almost Never   Sometimes   Often   Almost Always

During performance,
my hands shake .... Almost Never   Sometimes   Often   Almost Always

During performance,
my hands are cold .... Almost Never   Sometimes   Often   Almost Always

During performance,
I experience
shortness of breath.............. Almost Never   Sometimes   Often   Almost Always

During performance,
I experience
a fast heart beat.................. Almost Never   Sometimes   Often   Almost Always

During performance,
if I make a mistake, I panic .... Almost Never   Sometimes   Often   Almost Always

After performance,
I get very nervous................ Almost Never   Sometimes   Often   Almost Always

Once a student has thought about and talked about these responses, help prepare them to face these manifestations. Thoroughly examine their feelings about performing. Remember that inexperienced performers don't know what to think or expect. Talk with them (don't scare them) about performance expectations.

It cannot be stressed enough that the first and most important step in overcoming fear begins by making certain that preparation is thorough. Inadequate preparation and memorization are the greatest contributing factors to the appearance of performance anxiety.

Performance Anxiety Hints

Encourage students to address performance anxiety head-on and:
- Perform frequently for friends, parents and in the public.
- Seek opportunities to play for school, family, church, friends, and in contests and recitals.
- Avoid listening to other performers before the performance.
- Think and concentrate on the piece before the performance begins.
- Establish the tempo mentally before the performance begins.
- Listen during the performance.
- If *p* or *pp* passages are not sounding, be prepared to play louder.
- Think during the performance.
- Concentrate on the details of the phrases themselves.
- Stay focused and concentrate.

For further information regarding performance management see the following books:
- *The Art and Technique of Performance* by Richard Provost
- *Taking Centre-Stage: How to Survive and Enjoy Performing in Public* by Ruth Bonetti
- *Performance Success: Performing Your Best Under Pressure* by Don Greene and Julie Landsman
- *Confident Music Performance* by Barbara Schneiderman
- *The Inner Game of Music* by Barry Green and W. Timothy Gallwey
- *A Soprano on Her Head* by Eloise Rispad

8.2.3 Microphone Technique and Considerations

Most local venues selected for studio recitals will have sound systems. The technical considerations of a sound system are countless and often complicated. The concern is that amplification, microphones, stands, cords, and cables become a compliment to, and not a distraction from the performance. Hire a sound specialist, if need be, so technical considerations do not detract from the performance.

Every teacher will use a microphone at some point. Many times adults do not know how to use microphones properly and subsequently their students use them improperly as well. Microphone technique should be shared with students through demonstration and practice.

Guidelines for microphone technique include:
- Get close enough to the microphone for it to pick up the sound.
- Encourage students to become familiar with how they sound on the mic, so they will not be startled. Allow them to practice by announcing their names, addresses, *etc.*
- Warn students about feedback: its causes and cure.
- Microphones, stands, cords, and cables should become a compliment to, and not a distraction from the performance. The appropriate mic height for any situation except a rock concert is just slightly below the chin. Tip the mic up to about a 45 degree angle toward the mouth. Otherwise, raise or lower the adjustable portion of the stand with one hand while tightening with the other. Never bend down to try to speak "into" the mic; speak "across" it to the audience.
- If the mic needs to be taken off the mic stand, students should know ahead of time what kind of clip attaches it and rehearse removing it and replacing it in one natural motion.
- In a duet at a single mic, each performer sings to the two-thirds of the audience who are across the mic from them. The audience perceives the couple not as individuals, but as a single unit. Psychologically, the overlapping focus does reach out to the entire audience from the unit.
- The singer on stage-right will necessarily ignore the people over his right shoulder, knowing that his partner is including them in her focus. Both singers/speakers should take advantage of non singing moments to include that off-mic audience in their forum. Turning away from the mic while singing destroys the music which has been diligently prepared.

In all venues, supply these basics:
- low-impedance microphone
- mic cable
- XLR-to-1/4 inch transformer

Consider a basic model like the Shure SM58 for a first microphone purchase. It costs around $100 and will work in all kind of live performance situations. The well-adjusted, well-chosen mic will pick up the inflection or the intensity that is projected from any performer.

8.3 Thematic Events

Performing opportunities need not solely be recitals. Consider options in addition to solo recitals. Possible formats include:

- duet
- ensemble
- monster
- faculty

Investigate common as well as unusual options and remember the importance and benefits of ensemble as well as solo playing.

8.3.1 Program Themes

Thematic recitals are great for participants who are high-school-age and younger. Recital program themes add a different aspect to the preparation and performance of the event. Decide on the theme well in advance so appropriate repertoire can be selected, studied, and assigned.

Theme: **Musical Travel**
Take a musical journey around the world. Select repertoire that represents many different nationalities in both sound and title.

Decorations: Students could perform in costume. Design a power point for an overhead that includes a map showing the country of origin as well as pictures from the country as a particular piece is performed. Put flags and identifiable items from the country on the program as well as the stage.

Refreshments: Serve foods from other lands.

Theme: **The Colors of Music**
Select repertoire that has colors in the titles.
Invite an artist to do some sketching and/or talking about the use of color.

Decorations: Students could perform wearing the color of their piece.
Use multi-colored helium balloons to inexpensively decorate the stage. Paint a rainbow backdrop. Use multi-colors for the program cover.

Refreshments: Serve foods and beverages with unusual colors.

The Private Music Instruction Manual: A Guide for the Independent Music Educator • Rebecca Osborn

Theme: **Circus Time**
Gear this for younger students. Select repertoire with circus animal or activity titles. The beginning methods books (piano especially) have a host of them. Begin the recital like the Ringling Bros., with a big parade of participants.

Decorations: Students could perform in costume. Make the stage into a big-top that is open out to the audience. Put clowns, circus animals and a big-top on the front of the program.

Refreshments: Popcorn, peanuts and cotton candy are a must.

Theme: **A Musical Garden**
Select repertoire that has trees or flowers and nature inspiration in the title. Introduce each title with a description of what's presented in the piece. Use PowerPoint to show a picture of what is described in the song.

Decorations: Invite a local florist to decorate for free publicity. Or, ask the local garden club to decorate.

Refreshments: Serve fruits and vegetables accompanied by various juices to drink.

8.3.2 Play-a-thon

Organize a play-a-thon for a needy student or situation in your community. This is a highly successful way to benefit many. Whether it be an event to save an endangered building, or a way to help an accident victim, or cancer patient, a play-a-thon is a gratifying and worthwhile event. The students, the recipient, and the studio all benefit.

Plan an event that will last from 6 to 24 hours. Require students to sign up in 15-30 minute increments as soloists or in ensembles. Have participants take sponsor names and pledge amounts before their event performance. Contact the local newspaper before the event, and ask for a reporter and photographer to cover a portion.

Thousands of dollars can be raised through this performing opportunity.

8.3.3 Battle of the Bands

Organize students into bands and ensembles who will perform in an "open-mic" atmosphere. Encourage groups to perform 2 or 3 pieces. Advertise and encourage the public to attend. This will serve as advertising for the studio as well as a positive performing experience for the students.

8.4 Advertising

This author lives in a small town in which the local newspaper would consider any recital newsworthy. Review the press release guidelines found in section 6.3.3 of this book. Always write a press release before and after a studio recital or performing event.

Practical Application

Write a sample press release announcing an upcoming studio-sponsored recital. Include all pertinent information as you would have it appear in the paper.

8.5 Teacher/Studio Preparation

Meticulous recital planning will insure the recital's success. Use the following information to organize a studio recital.

8.5.1 Six-Month Preparation

Six months before the recital:

1. **Secure a recital location.**
   - Seek a large enough location.
   - Seek a location within your budget.
   - Seek a location that carries liability insurance. Churches and schools are good options since they are large venues that carry insurance.

2. **Secure a light/sound person.**
   Plan to pay their hourly rate. This may be a large expense, but odds are it will be a necessity.

3. **Secure a performance accompanist, if necessary.**

4. **Announce the date and location to students.**

5. **Secure liability insurance for that date, if necessary.**
   Contact local independent agents to shop for who offers the most competitive price.

8.5.2 Three-Month Preparation

Three months before the recital (depending on the level of the students):

1. **Assign recital repertoire.**

2. **Make a second announcement of the date and location to the students.**

3. **Remind students, if required, that recital music should be memorized.**

8.5.3 One-Month Preparation

One month before the recital:

1. **Determine recital programming**
   As the program order in which the students will perform is determined, work to present material by principles of balance, unity, contrast, and variety, paying attention to keys, composers, period, theme, as well as the ability level of the performers. Not all of these evaluations can be determined simultaneously, so once it is determined which concepts will be utilized for organization, decide on programming. Traditional rules of programming follow an inverse bell-shape. Set the most memorable performances for the opening and closing spots.

2. **Determine:**
   - if traditional rules of programming will be followed.
   - if the program will be programmed by accelerated ability levels.
   - if another format will be chosen.
   - where you want the peak to occur.

3. **Ask students if they have any needs regarding the particulars of where in the program they will perform.**
   For example, "my mom has to go to work, so may I please be placed toward the beginning of the recital?" (These requests may affect and determine programming.)

4. **Advertise/announce to students and parents.**
   Generate an announcement on paper to be handed out to students, to be posted at the studio, and to be sent out in the form of an email. (Be prepared, even with this level of saturation, there will still be those who are unaware of the date, time, and location and will attempt to blame your inability to communicate for their lack of knowledge.)

5. **Write a press release announcing the recital for the local paper.**
   If the recital is an opportunity for an outstanding student to publicly be selected, or a presentation to be made for achievement, then trophies, certificates and awards should be ordered.

8.5.4 Two-Week Preparation

Two weeks before the recital:

1. **Plan for refreshments at the recital.**
   Ask families for help. Post refreshment sign-up sheets and encourage participation. Let people know what the studio will supply and give them a list of what they could bring.

2. **Review recital etiquette and dress.**

3. **Discuss warm-up time and location.**

4. **Publish and post the directions to the recital location.**
   • Make maps available.
   • Supply students with written information if needed.

5. **Purchase paper for programs if they will be done on a studio copier or secure the best price/location for programs to be printed.**

8.5.5 One Week Preparation

One week before the recital:

1. **Post the program prototype so last-minute additions and corrections can be made.**
   It is possible to forget someone, this way the students will check for their own names and selections.

2. **Copy and fold the programs at least two days prior to the recital.**
   A good rule of thumb for the number of programs is to copy 4 times more programs than the number of recital participants.

3. **Programs**
   • Front cover should include studio name, your name, date, time, and location.
   • Inside should include students name, instrument, selection, and composer.
   • Any awards and special recognitions that will take place should be mentioned.
   • Any applicable "thank you" messages should be included.

4. **Plan the narration**
    - Will you announce each performer?
    - Will you have a student master of ceremonies?
    - Will each student announce themselves and their piece?
    - Will you or the students announce the welcome and closing statements?
    - Will performances run from one performer to the next without any announcement?

5. **Purchase any food or drink that will be served for refreshments.**

6. **Purchase any paper products and/or utensils that are needed for refreshments.**

7. **Purchase any decorations that will be used.**

8. **Ask someone to be a designated photographer/videoagrapher.**

9. **Prepare a recital program for the sound/light person marking any particular and specific requirements.**

10. **Prepare certificates and awards.**

11. **Secure a student to pass out programs.**

12. **Secure someone to serve drinks and refreshments.**

13. **Secure someone to help with clean-up after the recital.**

Practical Application

Select five pieces of typical intermediate-level repertoire for your instrument.

1. Decide the most outstanding feature of each of the repertoire selections.
2. Program the five pieces using the inverse bell format.
3. Program the five pieces using the accelerated format.
4. Write a prototype program incorporating:
    - program cover
    - student name
    - selection/composer name
    - announcements/pertinent information
    - special thanks section

8.5.6 At the Recital

At the recital:

1. Oversee the smooth running of this event.

2. Give any background tapes or CD's that are being used to the sound person.

3. Set up the stage with piano, stands, mics, and chairs in their appropriate location.

4. Set up the refreshment location before the performance.

5. Award student participants certificates.
    See Appendix H for a sample Recital Certificate.

5. Write down the time the recital began and ended.
    Take notes on anything that goes well, as well as anything that doesn't.

6. Do any necessary clean-up.

8.5.7 The Week After the Recital

The week after the recital:

1. Send thank-you notes to helpful parents, photographers, and anyone who aided in the recital's success.

2. Send a thank-you, check and/or some sort of gift to the sound person.

3. Write a press release and send to normal locations regarding the recital.

4. Use any pictures that are available.
    Remember to have a permission waiver signed for the students who will be used in conjunction with the press release.

5. Send checks and pay bills as necessary.

6. Put together a file folder with notes on everything associated with the recital. This will be very helpful for the future.
    See Appendix I for a recital timeline checklist.

8.6 Summary

One of the primary goals of private instruction is teaching the art of performance. It is for this reason, that recitals are an expected aspect of private music instruction. Students reap countless benefits from preparing and ultimately presenting a piece to an audience. Students and parents alike should be reminded that the ability to survive and perform in front of a crowd nurtures the kind of poise that is required in countless vocations.

However, the very thought of a recital will terrorize some students. Help them confront their performance fear and anxiety by analyzing, discussing, and seeking paths to prevention. Help students be prepared for the technical and physical aspects of a performance such as microphone technique and stage etiquette as well.

Consider themed, adult only, or charity recitals in addition to, or in place of the traditional.

Study the preparation guidelines in this chapter to aid in all facets of recital preparation.

CHAPTER 9

Legal Issues, Taxes, & Insurance

9.1 Legal Issues, Taxes, and Insurance

An independent music educator is self-employed. Being self-employed is significantly different from being an employee. A self-employed person must take all tax initiatives themselves. Failure to report teaching income can result in criminal and civil penalties. Penalties can include the forfeiture of money or time in prison, depending on the nature and severity of the violation. The independent music educator's knowledge of legal issues is imperative.

There is a complicated legal maze surrounding the operation of independent music studios. This chapter is a guide to addressing some legal questions. Please remember that this is only a guide. Due to the complexity of these legalities, it is in your best interest to hire professional assistance. The importance of enlisting the guidance of an accountant or tax representative, an attorney, and an insurance agent can not be overemphasized.

The intent of this chapter is to offer practical advice, not to dispense legal consul. This information is based upon the experience of this author and is provided only as a service to the reader.

Seek the help of an:

Attorney in order to:
- check on zoning and permit requirements.
- recommend the business structure.
- serve as your representative if legal action is taken against you.

Accountant in order to:
- explain tax laws and filing systems.
- file appropriate forms with the IRS.
- serve as your representative at an IRS ordered audit.

Insurance Agent in order to:
- suggest which insurance is best for your life and health insurance needs.
- suggest which insurance is best for your liability insurance needs.

9.1.1 Business Structures

There are 3 categories of small business structures: sole proprietorship, partnership, and corporation. In order to be a small business you must fall into one of these categories. Determining the structure of the business is the first legal step to take.

As a sole proprietor, whatever money the business earns is yours to keep. The business is you and you are the business. Most independent instructors opt to become sole proprietorships.

A partnership structure is obviously for duos who wish to set up their taxes collectively. Partnerships help provide a little more protection from personal liability.

There are advantages and disadvantages to incorporation. Proper incorporation will generally insulate the business owner from personal liability. Because of the complexities involved in this structure, an attorney should decide if this is advisable.

9.1.2 Independent Contractors

Frequently private music instructors will not set up their own business but will teach at someone's existing studio. If that studio does not take taxes out of money received, the government then considers these teachers independent contractors.

Professional assistance is also recommended even if establishing independent contractor status. Federal and state taxes are not withheld on behalf of independent contractors because they are considered self-employed and are treated as if they are running their own businesses.

To be an independent contractor, rent of teaching facility should be paid. The studio must let the IRS know the teacher earnings if they have exceeded $600 in a calendar year. The IRS then requires taxation on this income. Because the ordinary and necessary costs of operating a business are tax deductible, independent contractors can complete a Schedule C to deduct the full cost of most business expenses. See deductions listed later in this chapter.

9.1.3 Independent Teacher and Performing Musician

In the event that income is divided between two professional areas such as instruction and performing, the two careers should be kept separate. These two distinct activities require the filing of two different Schedule C forms.

9.2 The IRS and the SBA

The Internal Revenue Service and the Small Business Administration have recently established a small-business/self-employed division. They've created educational tools, a CD-ROM called The Small-Business Resource Guide and virtual CD-ROM, Small Business Workshop, and established a website specifically for the tax needs of the self-employed small-business owner. Order up to five copies for free at www.irs.gov/businesses/small.

Check the IRS website, www.irs.ustreas.gov. This is full of helpful tips and information. The site also provides instant access to important IRS forms and publications.

Call your local IRS office. Look in the white pages of the telephone directory under U.S. Government-Internal Revenue Service. Someone will be able to respond to your request for IRS publications and tax forms or other information. Ask about the IRS Tele-tax service, a series of recorded messages you can hear by dialing a touch-tone phone. If you need answers to complicated questions, ask to speak with a Taxpayer Service Specialist.

Obtain the basic IRS publications. You can order them by phone or mail from any IRS office; most are available at libraries and post offices. Start with Your Federal Income Tax (Publication 17) and Tax Guide for Small Business (Publication 334). These are both comprehensive, detailed guides. You will need to find the regulations that apply to you and ignore the rest. There are many IRS publications relating to self-employment and taxes. Publication 334 lists many of these publications, such as Business Use of Your Home (Publication 587) and Self-Employment Tax (Publication 533).

The Small Business Administration (SBA) provides a toll-free answer desk at 800-827-5722. This organization offers information on many educational, business development and loan guarantee programs. Their useful website can be found at www.sba.gov.

Do this research yourself. Be knowledgeable regarding the legal intricacies of this business. Then, set up an appointment with an accountant or tax attorney so they can explain and correct any errors or misconceptions.

9.3 Income Tax Estimates

When the business and tax structure have been established and reviewed by the accountant and/or attorney, ask him or her to offer advice and explanation regarding estimated income taxes.

A self-employed person does not have federal and state taxes withheld from their earnings. When taxes are not taken out of a paycheck or instructors are paid in cash, tax payments must be made by the self-employed individual directly to the IRS. These estimated taxes must be paid quarterly (4 times a year); on April 15, June 15, September 15, and January 15.

Persons who have never been self-employed are unaware of these circumstances since they have had no cause to be knowledgeable. This is another area where the tax professional should offer guidance. Many beginning private teachers become financially burdened simply because they don't realize that they must save money which will be used to pay their quarterly income tax payments.

To figure estimated tax, approximate adjusted gross income. Use form 1040-ES, Estimated Tax for Individuals, which includes a worksheet to aid in figuring estimated tax. IRS Publication 505 will also offer more information. If the estimated tax amount is less than $1,000, then quarterly estimated payments are not required.

Practical Application

Obtain form 1040-ES, Estimated Tax for Individuals, and using an annual projected income of $40,000, complete the form. How much money will you send to the IRS quarterly?

9.4 Social Security

For all self-employed individuals, Social Security and Medicare insurance taxes are combined. This figure changes periodically. Generally a tax rate of around 15% applies to the first $68,000 of net earnings from self-employment. No self-employment tax is payable if annual net earnings are less than $400.

9.5 Deductions

Self-employed individuals are eligible for many tax benefits that are not available when they are employees. These benefits come in the form of deductions. After the tax professional helps determine the business structure and establish the income tax filing system, ask him or her to explain all deductions that will be relevant to this business.

Deductions are government approved subtractions from business income. The rules and allowances regarding deductions change frequently. Make certain that deduction information that has been reviewed by the tax consultant is current.

The IRS requires documentary evidence to support expenditures of $75 or more. But to be on the safe side, collect receipts every time you incur an expense for the business.

As an independent music instructor, keeping accurate records of income and expenses is critical. Thorough records will facilitate the task of preparing a complete and accurate income tax return. They also serve to substantiate deductions in the event of an IRS audit.

Advanced legal record keeping need only be a change in thought process and personal organization. For example, save mileage logs, receipts, and cancelled checks so everything is documented and filed. This saving of paper is a behavior which must be learned. For information on how to keep records and how long to keep them, see IRS Publication 583.

Appendix J lists common deductions available to music educators who are sole proprietorships or independent contractors. Remember that each business situation is unique, and it is advisable to consult a tax professional to maximize deductions and minimize tax liability.

Business expenses fall into 4 basic categories:
- Studio location
- Travel, mileage, activities
- Insurance, dues, services
- Purchases

Review with your tax professional which expenses are deductible as well as what percentage should be calculated for each. For example, education expenses are 100% deductible while entertainment expenses are 50%. Some business expenses are considered direct while others are determined to be indirect. Once receipts are saved and categorized as in a Quick Books program, turn them over to the accountant. The tax professional will then determine what deductions are usable and their correct percentage deduction rates for a given year.

9.5.1 The Location

As discussed in Chapter 4, before a definite location for the business is selected, investigate local ordinances, licensing, and permit requirements to which an independent music instruction business will be subject.

For an in-home business, a house or part of a house must be used exclusively and regularly for the business in order for it to be itemized as a tax deduction. If teaching occurs in other locations but the home office is used for administrative or management purposes, then the office expenses are deductible.

Find the exact amount of the home bills which are deductible by dividing the expenses of operating the home between business use and personal use. Divide the area used for the business by the total square foot area of the home. This figure is the business percentage.

$$\frac{\text{Square footage of Business}}{\text{Square footage of the Home}} = \textbf{Business Percentage}$$

Exclusive use means that a specific part of the home is used only for the purpose of teaching. Regular use means that the studio uses that part of the home occasionally or incidentally. In order for an area of the home to be tax deductible, it must be used exclusively for the business. If the living room serves as a waiting room, then it can not be used as a deduction. If the house has been divided and has an exclusive area for the students, then all of that area and the expenses incurred therein are deductible.

Home is 2400 square feet; in-home studio is 800 square feet

This includes:
- exclusive waiting area
- exclusive studio
- exclusive rest room
- exclusive office

Then one-third of all home expenses are deductible.

That would include 1/3 of:
- mortgage
- rent
- utilities

If a store-front location is being used, expenses for rent, mortgage, insurance, utilities, and phone are 100% deductible business expenses. The home office expenses are deductible as well. See Appendix K for a sample floor plan which shows the percentage of studio space in a private residence.

9.5.2 Travel and Mileage

There are two possible calculation methods to determine deduction costs of business transportation.
1. The actual rate method.
2. The standard-mileage rate method.

The actual rate is determined by dividing:

$$\frac{\text{Number of miles driven for business purposes}}{\text{Total mileage, business and personal}} = \textbf{Actual Expense}$$

Actual expenses are the total expenses of the vehicle. These would include gas, oil, repairs, parking fees, tolls, insurance, depreciation, *etc*.

The standard-mileage rate is determined by multiplying:

$$\text{x} \quad \frac{\text{Number of miles driven for business purposes}}{\textbf{Your allowed deduction}} \quad \text{The standard mileage rate (32.5¢ for example)}$$

Have a tax professional determine what constitutes business miles in your particular situation. For example, if home is the principle place of business, generally, deductions can be taken for the cost of traveling from home to any business destination including mileage to and from the music or office supply store, a concert, a seminar, *etc*. If the regular office is outside the home, deductions may not be taken for the cost of commuting to or from that office, but deductions may be permitted for the cost of traveling to see students. A tax professional will know the specific answers to these questions.

When deducting business transportation costs, keep a mileage log and receipts detailing:

- Separate car expenditures
- Mileage for each business use of the car
- Date of business use
- Reason for business use
- Total annual mileage

This information will be filed on a Schedule C. See IRS Publication 917 for additional information.

9.5.3 Business Meals and Entertainment

To deduct expenses for business meals and entertainment, they must be shown to be ordinary and necessary to the business. The expenses must be directly related to the regular workings of the studio. A business meal is not deductible unless there is a substantial business discussion on a topic associated with the workings of the studio either before, during, or directly following the meal.

All business entertainment, from a Broadway show to an evening at a jazz club, are deductible expenses which are limited to 50% deductibility.

For all deductions keep a receipt from each expenditure showing:
- amount of the expenditure
- date of the entertainment
- place of entertainment
- description of entertainment
- business purpose and nature of the business benefit
- business relationship between the taxpayer and the persons entertained

9.5.4 Deductible Dues, Retirement Accounts, Insurance and Services

In order for goods and services expenses to be deductible, they must be ordinary and necessary to the studio. This would include categories such as professional service fees, professional organization dues, and professional publications.

Professional fees paid to lawyers and accountants are deductible in the year they are incurred. Bank fees are deductible as well.

Newspapers, journals, books, and music that are related to and necessary for the business are deductible. All music CD's as well as music instruction software are deductible. Magazine subscriptions are deductible if the reading materials are to be made available to the studio patrons in the waiting area.

Dues to professional associations and organizations such as MENC, ACDA, and MTNA are 100% deductible. These expenses should be reported on a Schedule C. If you incur these expenses as an employee and not as an independent contractor or sole proprietor use Form 2106 for these deductions as well as other employment-related expenses. See IRS Publication 529, Miscellaneous Deductions, for more information.

One of the greatest advantages available to the self-employed and independent contractor music instructor, is the ability to set up a tax-advantaged retirement plan. Earnings are not taxed until the account is drawn upon. A deduction can be taken at the time of the contribution in addition to tax-deferred growth. Seek the advice of an accountant or financial advisor to learn more about this.

In 2002, tax deductions for up to 70% of the health insurance premiums paid by self-employed musicians for themselves, their spouses, and dependents were permitted. The remaining portion of health insurance costs may be added to itemized medical expenses. This addition could help reach the necessary threshold of 7.5% of the adjusted gross income (AGI).

Educational expenses are 100% deductible. Life-time learning credit for college classes is offered to independent music instructors. See a financial advisor for advice on taking this opportunity as well.

9.5.5 Studio Equipment Purchases

Normally the entire cost of a piece of equipment cannot be submitted as a capital asset, business deduction for the year in which it was purchased. The amounts paid or incurred for the acquisition of assets that will remain useful for more than a year may not be taken as a deduction in one year. If an immediate deduction is not taken then it can be spread out over a number of years through depreciation. A tax consultant will be able to advise the best deduction alternative. The same rule applies to repair expenditures that appreciably prolong the life or enhance the value of existing assets. Expenditures must be capitalized and recovered through depreciation allowances over the life of the asset, if the asset is depreciable. If the asset is not depreciable, the cost is not recoverable.

Section 179 of the tax code presents the allowance of a depreciation in an amount of up to $24,000 for work-related equipment if the asset was purchased in a tax year since 1998. (So...go ahead and buy that Steinway!) This provision provides an immediate deduction, rather than one spread out over a number of years. The maximum amount that may be expensed under Section 179 can be determined by studying IRS Publication 946 for limitations and additional information and seeking the guidance of a tax professional.

Pens, paper, music, and literally hundreds of other little items used to keep the business running can be deducted as office supplies and business expenses. Basically, the supplies and equipment listed in Chapter 5 of this book are deductible. Studio expenses translate to tax deductions.

If a computer or television is going to be used primarily for the business but still used for personal use, the total cost of depreciation must be divided. There are limits on the depreciation deduction that can be claimed for a computer not used more then 50% in business use. Depreciation for a computer is over five years and seven years for a piano. See IRS Publication 946 for additional information.

The best time of year to purchase a major piece of equipment depends upon the individual tax situation. The decision is determined by whether the purchase will be expensed under Section 179 or depreciated over its useful life. Once again, consult a tax adviser as to when the purchase should be made.

When depreciating an asset of studio equipment under the Modified Accelerated Cost Recovery System (MACRS), a six-month convention is generally used. The MACRS places tangible personal property in either the three-year, five-year, seven-year, or ten-year class with a choice between the straight-line or 200%-declining-balance method, or in the fifteen-year or twenty-year class with a choice between the 150%-declining-balance or straight-line method. To determine which method provides the best tax advantage for studio purposes, examine the overall tax situation with a tax professional.

9.5.6 Not-for-Profit

Many studios opt to become a not-for-profit business. A not-for-profit corporation is one specifically formed for purposes other than operating a profit- seeking business, such as a charitable, religious, educational, or scientific purpose. There is, however, a mistaken belief that all "non-profits" cannot make money. Many not-for-profit studios function on grants and donations, their own charitable activities, or from ways unrelated to the non-profit purposes.

For purposes of incorporating, a non-profit is similar to setting up a regular for-profit corporation and would enjoy some of the same common features and benefits. Talk with a tax professional and other not-for-profit business owners to see if this is an option for your studio.

9.5.7 Book Sales

If music books will be sold to students, decide how those sales will take place.

Studios handle the sale of books and music in varying fashions. Some possible options include:
- Collect a book deposit at the beginning of the year. If students don't use the full amount during that year, then all remaining money is refunded back to them at the end of the year.
- Require the students to purchase their own books.
- Apply for a sales tax number in order to sell books. With this number, wholesale accounts can be established in the studio name. Sales tax must be collected and paid quarterly or annually.

Most music stores offer a 10% discount to teachers. Many book stores offer a 10% teacher discount.

9.6 Records

The importance of thorough business records cannot be over-emphasized. Keep good honest books. Investigate the use of a computer program such as Quick Books. These programs produce transactions that can be used for end-of-the-year tax documentation.

The IRS requires a business to keep records 3 years after they are filed, but 5 years is a good, safe rule of thumb. Don't pay cash for studio equipment and supplies unless absolutely necessary.

Business Records Guidelines

- A separate studio checking account should be maintained.
  - always put the date paid and check # on your receipts and bills
  - balance the checkbook monthly
- A receipt book for all business transactions should be used.
- A studio credit card account for business exchanges should be used.
- A log in a purse or glove compartment should be kept to record travel miles.

Appendix J and the chosen business application will help in determining what receipts to keep. These same categories should be set up in the computer tax program that is selected for the business.

Practical Application

Keep copies of all personal receipts for two weeks time. Separate the ones which will be deductible for your in-home music instruction business.

9.7 Insurance

Every business requires some form of insurance coverage and the studio is no exception. Insurance, while generally not as confusing as tax issues, can pose many questions that need to be answered by a professional.

When speaking to an insurance agent, be honest about the size and scope of the business. Disclose the number of students per week and annual gross income. If the studio is a sole proprietorship with a single instructor, most insurance companies will endorse the coverage needed to the homeowners' insurance police. A studio with multiple instructors will require a separate commercial policy. The insurance company will deny any claim they feel has been misrepresented in any way; therefore, make certain the agent fully understands the business needs.

Read the policy when it is received. Ask questions. **Don't assume anything.**

Several kinds of insurance are recommended to independent music instructors. Explore different types of insurance which may be essential for private music instruction.

9.7.1 Liability

Liability insurance will protect against "trip and fall" type incidents that may occur on the studio premises as well as liability suits that arise from the operation of the studio. Inquire as to whether "professional" liability coverage is included in a policy. A voice student could claim that instruction caused damage to vocal folds and only professional liability insurance would protect against that type of claim. The premium could be based upon the square footage of the studio, number of students, number of instructors, or annual gross income.

In some cases, a premises rider for a home-based business is all that is necessary for liability. However, if that is not sufficient, it should not be difficult to find a small-business insurance policy. In addition, it may be advisable to investigate an umbrella liability policy. For more information about the coverage a particular policy should contain, contact your state department of insurance.

The Private Music Instruction Manual: A Guide for the Independent Music Educator • Rebecca Osborn

If teaching occurs in an out-of-the-home location, speak with an insurance professional to confirm any liability insurance requirements.

Make certain that insurance is procured for recital and public performance locations that are utilized by the studio.

There may be opportunities to take students on a field trip. If this is an addition to the studio curriculum that will be pursued, extended auto insurance liability will be required. Ask an insurance professional for advice regarding transporting students.

All field trips should be accompanied by a signed parental permission slip which includes a liability waiver. The use of this slip will help protect you and the studio should any accident occur.

9.7.2 Personal Health

Health insurance is a costly component of self-employment. Premiums can be quite high. Shop around. Professional music organizations offer companies who cater to self-employed musicians. Investigate these options as well as insurance agents and companies in your neighborhood in order to get the most comprehensive coverage at the most competitive price.

9.7.3 Business Income and Extra Expense

This insurance will pay lost income in the event of a forced studio closure due to a covered loss. It will also cover loss or pay extra expenses to relocate for a short period of time while repairs are made.

9.7.4 Disability

Disability insurance is income protection which can generally protect for up to 60% of lost income. Look for non-cancelable, guaranteed renewable protection in the event you cannot work in your own occupation.

9.7.5 Property

Property insurance will protect your assets against direct causes of physical loss. When valuing the business personal property remember to consider the replacement value in determining the total amount of coverage needed.

9.8 Copyright and Fair Use

Copyright is a federal law which allows authors to control the use of their works for a limited period of time. Anything published less than 95 years ago is copyrighted if it carries a copyright notice. Anything published after March 1989 is copyrighted even without a copyright notice. Once that time period has expired, the public is allowed to freely use the works without paying royalties or obtained permission from the copyright holder. Copyright and copying issues should be studied and followed. Copyright and Fair Use Section 107, U.S. Code, Title 17 declares fair use standards for the copying of music. "Fair use" does not allow unrestricted copying, even for educational purposes. The purpose of the fair use exemption is to allow the public to use copyrighted works under certain circumstances without paying royalties or obtaining permission. Fair use is determined by applying a four-factor analysis that balances the rights of the copyright holder with that of the public.

Fair Use Four-Factor Analysis

First Factor: *The purpose and character of the use.*

Favors Fair Use	Favors Permission
Non profit	Commercial
Educational	For Profit
Personal	Entertainment
Teaching	
Criticism and Comment	
Scholarship and Research	
News reporting	

Second Factor: *The nature of the work to be used.*

Favors Fair Use	Favors Permission
Fact	Creative
Published	Unpublished

Third Factor: *How much of the work will be used?*

Favors Fair Use	Favors Permission
Small amount	Large amount

Fourth Factor: *Effect of the use on the market for the work.*

Favors Fair Use	Favors Permission
No effect	Major effect
Permission unavailable	Work is made available to the world

If the balance weighs in favor of fair use, then the work can be used without permission. However, if the balance weighs against fair use and other exemptions do not apply, then permission must be obtained to use the work.

The permissible uses of copyrighted materials include:
1. Emergency copying to replace purchased copies which for any reason are not available for an imminent performance provided purchased replacement copies shall be substituted in due course.
2. For academic purposes other than performance, single or multiple copies of excerpts of works may be made, provided that the excerpts do not comprise a part of the whole which would constitute a performable unit such as a section, movement, or aria, but in no case more than 10% of the whole work. The number of copies shall not exceed one copy per pupil.
3. Printed copies which have been purchased may be edited or simplified provided that the fundamental character is not distorted or the lyrics, if any, altered or lyrics added if none exist.
4. A single copy of recordings of performances by students may be made for evaluation or rehearsal purposes and may be retained by the educational institution or individual teacher.
5. A single copy of a sound recording (such as a tape or disc) of copyrighted music may be made from sound recordings owned by an educational institution or an individual teacher for the purpose of constructing aural exercises or examinations and may be retained by the educational institution or individual teacher.

Practical Application

Go to your personal music library and find a piece of photocopied music. Research the repertoire and recall the circumstances surrounding the acquisition of the piece. Are you using a listening or illegal copy? Why?

9.9 Small Claims Court

Unfortunately, at some point in this business, it's highly probable that a bad check will be written. It is also possible that someone will have received instruction and never paid for it at all. If either of these scenarios take place, some sort of collection must occur. See Appendix L for possible letters to send the parties involved.

Each county has different requirements for filing a claim against someone in small claims court. Travel to the county courthouse and find the small claims office. Bring copies of any and all paper work associated with this situation, and fill out forms to file charges. Be prepared to pay a cash filing fee, anywhere from $40-70. The defendant will be responsible for reimbursement of these court costs at the time of the court ruling in your favor. A future court date will be assigned and all paperwork will be forwarded to the defendant either in person by a sheriff, or in the mail as a certified letter.

Often a defendant will settle things up before they ever reach a court date. Sometimes, however, the defendant will not pay and will contest in court. You'll both appear before the judge on the assigned date and time and plead your cases.

If the defendant does not appear, then the case is automatically decided in favor of you, the plaintiff. It may still be difficult to collect the money from the defendant without another appearance in court in which the judge will garnish the defendant's wages and make arrangements for payments to be made to you.

Don't let the difficulty of filing a small claims court appeal deter you from collecting the money which is rightfully yours.

9.10 Summary

A self-employed independent music educator must be aware of legal, tax, and insurance requirements and seek the help of a qualified attorney, accountant, and insurance agent for advice on how to proceed.

The first legal step to take is to determine the structure of the business: sole proprietorship, partnership, or corporation. If operating as an independent contractor, determine how Federal and State taxes will be paid and what necessary operating costs are deductible such as studio rental. If the teacher operates as an independent instructor and performing musician, the two careers should be kept separate and two Schedule C's will need to be filed.

The IRS and SBA offer many helpful publications and CD-ROMs. Be knowledgeable regarding legal intricacies and then arrange for an appointment with an accountant or attorney.

Self-employed individuals are eligible for many tax benefits which come in the form of deductions relevant to the business. Review these deductions with a tax consultant. Use lists in the appendices of this text as well as information regarding business, location, and mileage to guide deductions.

Set up an IRA with the assistance of your financial professional. Seek insurance coverage for health, disability, liability, and homeowners (or property) under the advise of your insurance professional.

Copyright and copying issues should be studied and followed. Know the permissible uses of copyrighted materials.

Have paperwork in place for tuition collection and returned checks. Know the steps involved in taking legal action, if required.

CHAPTER 10
Studio Policies

10.1 Studio Policies, Parent Guides, and Evaluation

The writing and gathering of the documents presented in this chapter will conclude the studio case statement. At the time of their enrollment these forms should be given to each new student and family engaging your instruction and the services of your studio. Forms should be visually professional and their content should leave no room for question or dispute.

10.2 Studio Policies

For legal protection of the studio as well as for the professional outlook and ongoing successful performance of the business, all studio policies must be in print and made available to students and their families. Once any policy is in print it is copyrighted material and considered a legal document. The more legally binding and complete the documentation, the better protected the studio will be. When disputes arise, the private instructor's greatest ally is a thoughtfully-written set of policy documents. The most suitable method for policy to be enforced, is in the form of a contract.

10.3 Contract

The details and specifics of the studio contract are dependent upon the scope of the business. If the studio has students on a waiting list and instruction is in high demand, the contract can and should be exceedingly specific. The reason this specificity is required is due to the fact that the greater number of studio students will unfortunately be in direct proportion to the greater number of attendance and payment problems encountered.

More students = More attendance and payment problems

This is not to say, however, that the contracts for beginning teachers or small studios should not address attendance and payment policies in just as graphic and professional a manner as studios with larger numbers of students. Itinerate instructors need contracts as well.

It is highly desirable, from a legal standpoint, for the contract to be presented point-by-point; unfortunately, some people will not study or even skim through the documentation and thus may ultimately attempt to hold the studio responsible for their own failure to read. Dividing information by points allows for an easier-to-read format.

It is probably most effective to distribute contracts to returning students annually.

The contract should include:

1. **An opening paragraph or statement comprised of language that announces what is contained in the agreement.** This is the entire arrangement between the parties and it should state that there have been no oral or other representations or promises made that are not a part of this contract.

2. **The entire attendance policy and requirements.** Be thorough. Address canceled lessons, make-up lessons, at what time a lesson becomes a no-show lesson, student tardies, school closures, weather-related closures, teacher-generated cancellations, *etc.* And these requirements should be addressed regardless of the teaching location. Any lack of stated policy will be perceived as a lack of professionalism by the music-education-seeking public.

3. **The specifics of payment requirements.** This information should be spelled out in nauseating detail. Exactly what the payment is, when the payment is due, possible late fees and charges, amount charged for insufficient fund returned checks, and family discount rates. It should also be stated that in the event that a student must be taken to court due to lack of payment for services received, they are responsible for court and attorney costs and fees.

4. **The length of time involved in the relationship.** Are lesson contracts offered on a weekly, monthly, semester, or yearly basis? Address how much advanced notice either you or the student must give in order to terminate the teaching relationship. Leave room in the contract to exit this instructional situation. Indicate under what conditions either the student or the teacher can prematurely end the relationship and include a very explicit provision for unilateral dismissal of a student from instruction.

Exceptions to studio policies should rarely, if ever, be granted and, even then, only under extraordinary or singular circumstances. This lack of exception is the key to policy and contract success.

After a contract has been conceived and written and before it is instituted, keep in mind that if legal proceedings are warranted, anything that is unclear or ambiguous will be tossed out of court. The courts invariably interpret ambiguous terms against the person who drafted the contract.

Therefore, as with all studio materials, make sure thorough proofreading takes place and if finances allow, ask a legal advisor to peruse and alter the contract language.

Require the financially responsible individual to read the studio policies and to sign two copies of the contract. The individual should keep one signed contract copy and the other should be kept for studio records.

Practical Application

Look at the following contracts and policies. These are actual documents from studios around the U.S. Are the policies worded in a clear and concise manner? Address the flaws in the contracts and policies by discussing and/or listing at least three possible problems or omissions.

Policy Example #1

Fees are payable monthly, in advance. Payment is due on the last lesson of the preceding month.

Voice $35 per 40 minutes
Piano $22 per 30 minutes

Lessons will be paid for in advance by the month. Payment is due on the last lesson of the preceding month.

One month's notice must be given prior to termination of lessons. NOTE: If you miss a lesson and do not call with an explanation, your lesson time will not be guaranteed thereafter.

No allowance will be made for lessons missed or canceled by students (except by special arrangement in cases of prolonged serious illness). There are no make-ups and no credits for missed or canceled lessons.

In the event of the teacher's absence, an adjustment will be made.

Time lost because of a student's lateness cannot be made up.

The Private Music Instruction Manual: A Guide for the Independent Music Educator • Rebecca Osborn

Policy Example #2

Private Lessons

Lesson Time & Payments:

A half hour private lesson will be held at the same time and day each week. Lessons are by appointment only, $96 per month (whether there are 4 or 5 lessons). Hour long lessons can be arranged. All lesson scheduling and rescheduling takes place at the front desk. Tuition for lessons is due at the advance. If payment is not received by the 15th of the month, lessons will be suspended.

On months with holidays (including a 5 week month), when you receive 4 lessons you will be charged the regular monthly fee (holidays will not be made up). When there are less than 4 lessons, you will be charged the single lesson price for the remainder of the month.

Weekly payments can be arranged at $24 per lesson (months with 5 lessons will cost you $120). Weekly payers are expected to pay for all lessons—including absences—in order to maintain the time slot.

As a courtesy to the teacher, we request 3 days notice if you decide to stop your lessons. You will be considered a student on our schedule until we are notified of a change.

Student Absences:

With 24 hours' notice of the cancellation, one rescheduled lesson per month is offered as a courtesy. The time can only be made up within the month following the cancellation. Rescheduled lesson times are solely based on the teacher's availability.

Canceled make-ups cannot be rescheduled.

Teacher Absences:

In the event of absence by your usual teacher, a highly qualified substitute will be provided whenever possible. If a substitute teacher isn't available you will receive a credit ($21) toward your next month's tuition.

Student Obligation:

It is the responsibility of the student to arrive at the lesson on time with his/her instrument as well as all books needed for the lesson.

Bad Weather:

Call the studio. There will be a message on the answering machine.

Holidays:

Our lesson schedule does not follow your school calendar. Private lessons will not be held on New Year's Day, Memorial Day, Independence Day, Labor Day, Thanksgiving, or Christmas Day.

Policy Example #3

LESSON POLICY

LESSON PAYMENT, CANCELLATION, AND RESCHEDULE POLICIES:

1. Lessons must be paid for at the first lesson date of each month, for the entire month in advance. The first lesson is the grace period; if payment is not made by the second monthly meeting, that and subsequent meetings will be canceled until the account is brought up to date.
2. 24 hours notice is required to cancel a lesson, with Monday cancellations to be made by 12 noon. One cancellation per month will be permitted, with the prepaid fee being applied to the following month's bill. Alternatively, a make-up lesson may be scheduled (at the discretion of the individual teacher).
3. Make-up lessons must be rescheduled with the teacher within 30 days.
4. No cancellation credit will be given for time which has not been paid for in advance, or for which cancellation and/or rescheduling have not been made in a timely manner, as set forth above.
5. If the professional staff is forced to cancel a lesson, there will be NO LOSS to the student. If a make-up lesson time cannot be arranged, credit will be applied towards the following month's fee.

INCLEMENT WEATHER CLOSINGS:

The studio will be closed if the local school systems are closed, unless other arrangements are made with the teacher.

About The Music Lessons:

Lessons are $60 per month, payable upon the student's first lesson each month. The sessions are one-half hour each week, four lessons each month ($15 per lesson). Lessons may not be paid individually or partially; the fee of $60 must be paid in full on the first lesson each month. [If the student's lesson day has five in a month, one of the lessons will be omitted, always guaranteeing every student four lessons each month.] If the student cancels a lesson at anytime for any reason, a credit or refund will not be given; a make-up will be given only if time permits, at the teacher's discretion. If a lesson is canceled for any other reason or by the teacher, a make-up will be scheduled or a credit given. NO REFUNDS.

Lessons will be offered weekdays during the afternoon and early evenings.

The first lesson is offered FREE as a "Get-To-Know" session for both student and teacher!

The Private Music Instruction Manual: A Guide for the Independent Music Educator • Rebecca Osborn

Policy Example #4

Private music lessons at the cost $65 in monthly tuition.

By signing this statement you are demonstrating your understanding and agreement to abide by studio payment policies and procedures.

Monthly tuition is due at the first lesson of each month. This monthly tuition remains the same from September through May regardless of the number of lessons in the month.

A late fee of $5 will be assessed to any tuition that is not paid by the 15th of the month.

Price exceptions will be granted to families with 3 or more members enrolled in weekly private lessons. This three lesson discount is 6.7%.

If the monthly tuition is not paid in full by the last day of the month, lessons will be suspended for the following month and the lesson time will be forfeited. In the event of a financial or personal emergency, an exception to the suspension may be granted if handled in the following manner:

The student or parent must inform the studio of the emergency.

A payment plan must be agreed upon by both parties prior to continued instruction.

1. For musical growth and escalated learning to occur, regular lesson attendance is required. Students are encouraged to trade with other students so that a lesson is not missed. A lesson trade may also be made if the teacher has an available open lesson time during the week of the conflict. Cancellations by the student will not be credited. As a courtesy to the teacher, students are requested to give a call to the studio at least three hours prior to lesson time if they will not be attending.
2. Cancellations made by a teacher will result in a credit to the student's next monthly tuition payment if a substitute teacher has not been provided.
3. Students must pay any previous balances prior to beginning a new year of study.
4. Students will be considered delinquent after two consecutive no-call/no-show lessons, and will be suspended from lessons. Since the instructor is paid for no-call/no-show lessons, the student will be billed for them. In the event that the student terminates instruction mid-month, full tuition charges will still be assessed. Both the teacher and the office manager must be notified of lesson termination.
5. There will be a $20 charge assessed to any returned check.

I have read and fully understand the tuition payment policies of the Studio. My signature signifies my agreement to pay monthly tuition and any additional late fees that I may incur under this policy.

Signed_____ Date_____

Policy Example #5

MUSIC SCHOOL LESSON POLICY

LESSON RATES: All Private Instrument Lessons are $16 per half hour. Voice Lessons are $20 per half hour. Payment for lessons are paid monthly and are due on the first lesson of each month. Lesson payments received after the first lesson of the month will be charged a LATE FEE OF $5. Students who cancel the 1st lesson of the month are required to pay their lesson payment by the 8th of the month to avoid the late fee.

Lesson payments are nonrefundable and nontransferable.

CANCELLATIONS: The studio requires a one day advance notice if a student is not able to attend their scheduled lesson. Sick cancellations must be left on the studio answering machine prior to the studio opening. In the event of a teacher's absence, the Music Center will contact the student and arrange a make-up lesson at a further date.

MAKEUP LESSONS: The studio will provide a make-up lesson only if the cancellation requirements are met. Make-up lessons will be scheduled according to the teacher's availability. Canceled scheduled make-up lessons will result in the loss of the lesson and will not be rescheduled. We will allow up to 4 make-up lessons per year per student. The Music Center is not required to make up any more lessons after the maximum amount has been reached.

SCHOOL VACATIONS: The studio teaches lessons on all school vacations on our regular schedule and regular policy applies.

SUMMER VACATIONS: The studio teaches lessons all year long. Enrolled students are required to pay for the full month of June. Students who take lessons in July and August are not required to pay for lessons if they are on vacation. Please give advance notice.

HOLIDAYS: There are no lessons on the following holidays: NEW YEARS DAY, MARTIN LUTHER KING DAY, PRESIDENTS DAY, PATRIOTS DAY, MEMORIAL DAY, INDEPENDENCE DAY, LABOR DAY, COLUMBUS DAY, VETERANS DAY, THANKSGIVING, CHRISTMAS EVE, and CHRISTMAS DAY.

WEATHER CANCELLATIONS: In the event of a snowstorm, call the studio to see if we are still having lessons. If the studio remains open, regular policy applies. If the studio decides to close due to bad weather, students will be contacted and a makeup lesson will be scheduled at a further date.

RECITALS: The studio holds annual student recitals in late June. Students must be enrolled in our lesson program for the entire school year in order to participate.

Print Name: _____

Agreed to: _____ Date:_____

10.3.1 Student Contracts

Many teachers have found pleasantly surprising results from a student/ teacher contract. Students often take the act of signing a contract as quite a serious responsibility.

Contracts can be specific in the spelling out of instructor requirements, or open ended, as they encourage students to establish their own practicing criteria.

I, _____, agree to...

Possible inclusions addressed:

Amount of time spent on assigned materials.

Physical lesson preparation such as attendance, promptness and bringing of materials.

Number of excused practice days per month
i.e. Will not practice on Sundays.

Specific goals
i.e. Will complete this level of the
instructional method series in _____ amount of time.

Will perform _____ times in public in _____ amount of time.

Will memorize _____ pieces in _____ amount of time.

_____
STUDENT SIGNATURE

_____
TEACHER SIGNATURE

10.4 How to Dismiss a Student

Eventually, every teacher is faced with the need to end an instructional relationship. By having preexisting criteria, this problem can be dealt with in a professional manner.

Rather than dismiss in a fashion which may be perceived as abrupt or unprofessional, use a probationary system. Notify both student and parent of the impending dismissal. This can be done by phone, in person or in writing. Refer to student progress reports and comment on student performance and preparation rather than character or aptitude. Suggest also that this problem may well be the result of a personality clash or conflict. Be prepared to offer names of colleagues in the area as other possible instructor options.

> *Steps to dismissal:*
> 1. Announce the possible dismissal to the student and/or parent.
> 2. Offer a month of continued study and then a reevaluation.
> 3. Give the parent weekly verbal evaluations if they request.
> 4. At the one month point, confirm this less-than-abrupt decision to dismiss.

Dismissal can obviously be an uncomfortable situation. Strive for closure that demonstrates integrity and standards rather than a lack of patience and professionalism.

10.5 Parent/New Student Guides

As a component of the case statement, the use of guides and handbooks is recommended to introduce new students and their families to programs, performance opportunities, and services which are offered and sponsored by the studio. Organize the segments of the guide into a printed form, and as previously stated, present it to the student and/or the financially responsible adult at the first scheduled lesson meeting.

The parent guide should include:
- **Philosophy/mission statement**—information which was compiled in Chapter 1 of this text
- **Studio pamphlet**—a brief professional overview and contact information
- **Tuition/attendance policy and contract**—the contract (which was created earlier in this chapter)
- **General studio information**—guidelines, rules, incentives and etiquette
- **Parent guide for beginning students**—specific help to students and parents regarding practice on new instruments (see Appendices M, N, and O).
- **Schedule/Calendar of annual events**
- **Teacher/staff résumé**

10.5.1 Studio Rules, General Information, & Recital Etiquette

The general information guide or handbook will contain additional details pertaining to instruction at the studio. This would be located under the heading of general studio information in the new student/parent guide and would contain guidelines, rules, incentive information and etiquette.

Some possible inclusions
- entrance procedures
  - security gate
  - parking
  - ring or walk in
- storage of coat and shoes
- hands clean
- nails clipped
- student waiting area procedures
- computer/technology time procedures
- lending library procedures
- practice procedures
- reward policies
- summer lesson procedures
- parent/teacher conferences
- how and when to contact you
- progress reports and forms
- student evaluations

Itinerate Lesson Procedures
- no phone calls during lessons
- televisions should be turned off
- siblings and pets not allowed during the lesson

Recital Procedures
- mandatory or elective participation
- registration/participation fees
- music memorization required or not
- appropriate attire
- pianist shoe heel height

Recital Etiquette
Many families are not familiar with basic recital etiquette. Perhaps include a comment such as:
> *"All students deserve the courtesy of an attentive audience. Please make every effort to attend the entire recital as a consideration to all performers and remain politely quiet."*

10.5.2 Teacher or Staff Résumé

An additional fulfillment of the case statement is the résumé and history portion. This is the opportunity to share personal experience with prospective students. Parents are generally very interested in this information. It is more professional to include this in the form of a résumé rather than in a paragraph form. Teaching experience should be mentioned as well as the history (if any) of the business itself. If the studio has more than one instructor, include their résumés as well.

A *vitae* is not necessary, however, in the event that the business is just beginning, there may be a need to include as much as possible in this category.

Also include ongoing professional development such as further degree-seeking, membership associations, seminars, workshops, and subscriptions to music education magazines.

Expectations should be offered as a final portion of the résumé.

Let the patron know what they can anticipate from you, the instructor:
- Teacher will practice regularly.
- Teacher will maintain professional standards by studying and attending classes, workshops, concerts, and conventions.
- Teacher will be aware of current teaching materials, trends, changes, and methodologies in the field.
- Teacher will present timely, professional instruction.

Practical Application

Write a General Studio Information Guide.

Address and include at least seven procedures that you deem important for students to know and understand.

10.6 Evaluation

An equally important fulfillment of the case statement is evaluation. Evaluation is necessary both for the student and the instructor. The way a student shows improvement is by analyzing and modifying in response to instructor criticism and comment. As instructors, and as individuals, it is often difficult to take criticism. However, just as we expect our students to take correction and learn from it, we too should do the same. And who better to judge instructor performance than someone who is subject to it? The students.

10.6.1 New and Transfer Student Evaluation

Many teachers conduct an entry level evaluation in the form of an interview, a playing assessment, or both. Decide whether this will be a free service or if a consultation fee will be charged.

Before the interview occurs, try to find out if the prospective student has any learning disabilities, physical disabilities, or behavioral disorders. Most parents will offer this information at the inquiry phone call.

Use the representative Student Inventory Evaluations for piano and voice in Appendices P and Q as possible options.

Other potential inclusions:
- Years studied
- Information regarding former teacher, *i.e.* education, professional memberships, *etc.*
- Methods used
- Supplementary material used
- Music or musicians in the students' home

Performance audition
- General comments
- Singing
- Rhythmic response (clap, *etc.*)
- Note recognition
- Melodic patterns, sight-singing
- Ear testing: major/minor, scales, arpeggios, technique
- Additional comments

Practical Application

Using the samples in Appendices P and Q and the above list of possible inclusions to design an original transfer student evaluation form. Use questions which pertain to your instrument, your studio, and your priorities.

10.6.2 Student Evaluation

In order to monitor progress as well as materials assigned, it is often helpful to keep a notebook, computer file, or file folder on each student. Many private instructors even assign a weekly lesson grade. Contemplate use of a progress report or student evaluation and deciding which students will receive written evaluation; school-age students, elementary school-age students, or all students. Most people are accustomed to evaluation. It's a part of everyday living. Make certain that the chosen evaluation procedure is presented upon enrollment in the general information portion of the new student guide. This will insure student preparedness so there is no surprise when written evaluation occurs.

Once the specific group of students receiving evaluation are selected, decide how often and in what form these evaluations will take place.

Decide what form student evaluations will take:
- Progress Reports
- Report Cards
- Individual Lesson Evaluations
- Performance Evaluations
- Parent/Teacher Conferences

Decide what standard the chosen evaluation will take:
- Grades
- Numbers
- Categories
  - outstanding
  - excellent
  - good
  - average
  - needs improvement

Decide when the chosen evaluation will be distributed:
- Monthly
- Quarterly
- Semi annually
- Annually

Practical Application

Make a Progress Report form for your studio. Consider using some or all of the following categories:

- **Technique**—hand/mouth/body position, accuracy and dexterity, scales
- **Musicality**—phrase, artistry
- **Reading**—note recognition, rhythmic accuracy, phrasing, dynamics
- **Extensions**—improvisation, harmonization
- **Theory and Fundamentals**—keys, chords, transposition, aural skills
- **Preparation**—motivation, consistent practice, accurate practice, maintains practice log, completes written assignments, completes technology assignments
- **Lesson Commitment**—attendance, promptness, attentiveness, cooperation
- **Performance Evaluation**—preparedness, composure

In the interest of making the best use of instructor time, consider utilizing numerical or grade evaluations rather than blanks for each category. With the grade or numerical system only the categories which need improvement will warrant a written comment.

10.6.3 Student Evaluation for Further or Transfer Study

Often times a private instructor is requested to provide an evaluation for a transferring student or one bound for university study. Use progress report information to formulate this evaluation. Include also a list of representative literature and the method of instruction used.

10.6.4 Letters of Recommendation

Private music instructors are often called upon to write letters of recommendation. Write a few master templates and keep then on file. Specific information can be supplied regarding the length and capacity of the relationship with the student. Talent, musicality, technique, discipline, maturity, and aptitude for growth can also be addressed. In cases when you believe a recommendation is not warranted, have the courage to respectfully decline.

10.6.5 Student Self Evaluation

Many studios require an end-of-the-year student self evaluation. This can often prove more helpful to the teacher, than to the student.

Possible self-evaluation areas could include:
- **Practice evaluation**—scales, accuracy, dynamics, fingering, breathing, time commitment, motivation
- **Instruction responsiveness**—listens to teacher, reads teacher notes, asks questions, makes comments, attitude, attendance, promptness
- **Performance review**—preparedness, composure
- **I take lessons because...**

Practical Application

Create a student self evaluation form particular to your instrument and instruction.

10.6.6 Teacher Evaluation

One of the greatest forms of self-evaluation is videotape. Consider videotaping yourself teaching some lessons. This can be quite a learning experience. Be aware of how much talking you do and how much teaching is occurring. Notice pacing. Is too much time spent on one concept? Is there enough or not enough demonstration?

Consider also the use of a year-end teacher evaluation. This written review will serve to pin-point communication and educational problems or concerns and will ultimately aid and improve your instruction. Do a survey. Find out what people like or dislike about your service. Ask very specific questions. Questions will be answered with "yes," "no," or numerical ratings. Follow up questions with "Why?" where applicable. Leave a section for comments and suggestions. Use a different evaluation for students and parents. There will be a better response if the length of the evaluation does not exceed one page.

Sample Student Evaluation

The _____ Studio strives to provide the best possible music education for our students. By completing this brief evaluation, your input will aid in the continuation and betterment of the quality instruction we offer. Thank you for your time.

SA   Strongly Agree
A   Agree
D   Disagree
SD   Strongly Disagree

1. I think my teacher is fair and caring...............SA   A   D   SD

   Why?_____

2. I think my teacher is knowledgeable. ....SA   A   D   SD

   Why?_____

3. My teacher knows how to
   share knowledge. ....SA   A   D   SD

   Why?_____

4. My teacher makes learning interesting...........SA   A   D   SD

5. My teacher reviews and reinforces
   concepts and techniques as needed ....SA   A   D   SD

6. My teacher is prepared for lessons................SA   A   D   SD

7. My lessons have a good balance between
   talking and teaching and making music ....SA   A   D   SD

8. My teacher doesn't cheat my lesson time ....SA   A   D   SD

9. My teacher (circle one)...

   expects too much.   does not expect enough.   has realistic expectations.

Practical Application

Write a student evaluation personalized to your studio. Include a minimum of five questions relevant to your situation.

10.7 Summary

At the time of student enrollment, studio information forms should be given to each new student and family. Forms should be visually professional and their content should leave no room for question or dispute. This information is not only for the ongoing successful performance of the business, but is also for legal protection as well. The more legally binding and complete the documentation, the better protected the studio will have.

Many teachers have found positive results from a student/teacher contract. Students often take the act of signing a contract quite seriously and will work harder to succeed because of it.

Develop a parent guide that will present all information regarding the studio. The parent guide should include:
- Philosophy/mission statement
- Studio pamphlet
- Tuition/attendance policy and contract
- General studio information
- Parent guide for beginning students
- Schedule/Calendar of annual events
- Teacher/staff resume

Studio rules such as they apply to the facility, recitals, practice procedures, *etc.*

In order to monitor progress as well as materials assigned, it is often helpful to keep a notebook, computer file, or file folder on each student. Many private instructors even assign a weekly lesson grade. Contemplate use of a progress report or student evaluation. Have a form or guide to evaluate incoming beginner and transfer students. Consider the inclusion of a student self-evaluation as well.

Consider also the use of a year-end teacher evaluation. This written review will serve to pin-point communication and educational problems or concerns that will ultimately aid and improve your instruction.

CHAPTER 11

Time for Change

11.1 Time for Change

Everyone knows the adage, "If it ain't broke, don't fix it." The same can be said for the studio. Strive for constant improvement in all aspects of the business. Forward motion is crucial. But, by the same token, if something has worked and worked well, don't change it. Be wise enough to evaluate and astute enough to change. Policies, tuition, activities, methods, and basically any concept that this text book has helped your studio establish, can be changed. However, uncertainty may come in deciding exactly what to change.

11.1.1 Tuition Changes

An alteration that will be necessary and unpleasantly received is a change in tuition. This change will undoubtedly be a rise in tuition prices.

There are two indicators that justify a tuition increase:
1. Your roster is full. You have become so popular and sought-after that there are several names on your waiting list. If this is the case, then a tuition increase is warranted in the fall. A waiting list is a testament to studio quality and provides added assurance that if a student does quit because of the price increase, there will be someone ready to fill the vacancy.
2. You haven't raised your tuition in three years. Find out what the increase in the cost of living has been in that time. This increase should be reflected in studio tuition. Quote this number in the announcements to the students regarding the rise in tuition. Also, the improvements in your teaching in the last three years can alone justify this increase.

Raise the cost of tuition by numbers that are factors of five so the amount is always a nice and tidy sum.

11.1.2 Activity Changes

As part of the inauguration of the studio and in an effort to entice students into lessons, some activities may be a part of the curriculum that, two years later, have lost their effectiveness.

Individually examine each activity that the studio offers and those in which you or your students participate. Each audition, each competition, each festival, each recital, each incentive activity, each seminar, each convention...evaluate them all. Just because an activity was well received in the last community you lived, doesn't mean it will fair well in your new hometown. Evaluate and determine if each is a positive contribution to either the students or to you as a professional. Weed out the activities which are not providing sufficient return for the time, money, and effort invested.

11.1.3 Brochure and Printed Material Changes

So even after all the checks and double-checks it seems that something in the studio brochure is ambiguous. Prospective students and their families often seem to share confusion and ask the same questions.

Rather than reword and then reprint the studio brochure to answer recurring questions, consider making a FAQ (Frequently-Asked Questions) sheet to clarify information. This is a cost-effective solution. Wait and correct the information on the next printing of the brochures. Use the FAQ sheet as an additional means to present further detail regarding studio policies.

However, rather than scolding yourself for writing ambiguous policies, remember that the majority of the people just don't read the materials they're given.

11.2 Solo Business Becomes an Ensemble

So the business has become so successful that a first employee needs to be hired. Be prepared for this huge change. Life will become much more complicated. Even if the employee is just a part-time person brought in to help with billing and collection, be prepared for a shock. The biggest surprise for the first-time employer is the cost of adding even one employee. Employment taxes, benefits, and insurance can add 25 to 50% to the base wage. Sit down with an accountant and calculate these costs before a help-wanted ad is ever placed. There are tax forms and procedures which will need to be used in order to create a payroll. An accountant will explain these.

You are now a business person...yet another hat; not just a musician, not just an educator, now an employer and manager. Strive to continuously fine-tune management skills. Consider attending a class or workshop or reading reference materials that offer step-by-step instruction in the how-tos of being a boss.

Some possible books to aid in preparation for the growth of the business include:
- *The Boss's Survival Guide* by Bob Rosner, Allan Halcrow and Alan W. Levins; McGraw-Hill, 2001.
- *The Employer's Legal Handbook* by Fred S. Steingold; Nolo Press, 2001.
- *Growing Your Own Business: Growth Strategies for Meeting New Challenges and Maximizing Success* by Greg and Patricia Kishel; iUniverse.com, 2000.

11.2.1 Add Another Teacher

There are two employment options regarding adding a teacher to the staff; this person can be an employee or an independent contractor. The studio is responsible for the income taxes of its employees and therefore has the legal right to make requirements and requests of that person. An independent contractor is considered self-employed by the government and is therefore responsible for his or her own income taxes. Because of this relationship, the studio can make suggestions, but not requirements, of an independent teacher.

If a teacher is added to the staff, changes that may need to occur include:
1. **Organization of the workplace.**
   Since two or more people need to find books, equipment, or even the music dictionary, the studio will need a level of organization which may not currently exist.
2. **Creation of an employee manual and/or job description.**
   The staff needs to run things at existing studio standards. Write requirements, procedures and guidelines telling the employee exactly what's expected. Teachers that are independent contractors will need guidelines and not requirements since they are not legally employees of the studio. Offer the manual to an accountant or attorney to make certain that inappropriate language is not presented.

Written policies will provide freedom from inconsistencies. Guidelines and constructive communications are necessary.

When hiring, follow your instincts. More important than credentials is a person's educator mentality. Do they know how to impart their knowledge? Can they teach?

This person is going to be locked in a confined space with an under-age student for thirty minutes a week. Along with skills and aptitude, the virtue and ethics of this instructor should be above and beyond reproach.

Network fellow musicians and advertise at local musical haunts when seeking new instructors. Ask for a resume before ever granting an interview. A resume is extremely telling. Make sure to read between the lines as well as what's on the paper.

At the interview, watch for body language and eye contact. Is this a self-assured, comfortable person with a positive attitude?

Some sample lines of questioning might include:
- Examples of work history
- Review of education
- How theory is incorporated into a lesson
- Previous methods and repertoire taught as well as studied
- How to handle a disgruntled parent
- Favorite age to teach
- Favorite ability-level to teach
- How to handle an unmotivated student

Discuss pay, hours, taxes, and general expectations.

Encourage new teachers to watch some of the lessons you teach so they can get a feel for your instruction and demeanor.

Keep the lines of communication open by always taking suggestions and ideas under advisement. Acknowledgment of birthdays and other gift-giving holidays will be appreciated by any employee. Being a good employer is very much like being a good parent: listen, respect, then declare.

11.2.2 Office Manager

An office manager or secretary can be hired to be in charge of the day-to-day operations of everything except music instruction. The addition of this staff member would obviously provide the freeing of a considerable amount of instruction time and the time previously used for organization may now be used in the pursuit of a greater instructional income.

Possible office manager duties include:
- phone inquiries
- correspondence
- copying and compiling of all handbooks and guides
- music and supply ordering
- cleaning
- attendance and scheduling
- billing
- record keeping
- payroll

If you're not comfortable with an employee doing payroll and taxes, consider securing a payroll company or service. They will not only write checks or use direct deposit, but submit quarterly and annual tax forms as well. This service, which can be found on the internet, is often well worth the expense.

11.3 Self Maintenance

As the studio changes and grows so will anxiety, strain, and stress. Being a successful business person and a teacher can be overwhelming. Compound with personal obligations and there is very likely stress in the offing. Take time for yourself. Exercise, read, begin or maintain a hobby. Sometimes just time alone, sitting still, with minimal distractions can help with stress management and reduction.

Take steps early and often to ward off stress.

11.4 Summary

There are two indicators that justify a tuition increase. If your roster is full and a waiting list exists and/or if you haven't raised your tuition in three years.

Charge for your experience and expertise.

Often times questions are asked again and again. Rather than reword and then reprint the studio brochure to answer common reoccurring questions, consider making a FAQ (Frequently Asked Questions) sheet to clarify information. Wait and correct the details on the next printing of the brochures. The majority of the people simply do not read the materials they're given, regardless of how clearly the information is written.

If the business size and volume warrants, consider hiring an employee. Be prepared for a tremendous change. Strive to continuously fine-tune management skills as it's likely that life will become much more complicated. There are tax forms and procedures which will need to be used in order to create a payroll. Ask an accountant to explain these. There are two employment options regarding adding a teacher to the staff; this person can be an employee or an independent contractor. If a teacher is added to the staff, changes that may need to occur include organization of the workplace, as well as creation of an employee manual and/or job description. Guidelines and constructive communications are necessary. Written policies will provide freedom from inconsistencies.

When hiring, follow your instincts. More important than credentials is a person's educator mentality. Keep the lines of communication open by always taking teacher and colleague suggestions and ideas under advisement.

As the studio changes and grows so will anxiety, strain, and stress. Take steps early and often to ward off stress.

Practical Application

Look at possible questions in Section 11.2.1, to aid in interviewing a potential instructor.

Ask them about the particulars regarding their instrument and find out about their personal philosophy of education. The interview process should be specific enough to determine the suitability of this instructor and their ability to align themselves with your studio.

Put the questions in a logical order to be presented at an interview.

CHAPTER 12
D.C. al Fine

12.1 *Fine* (The End)

What is the most important thing a student should take away from your studio? What is your most important function as a teacher?
Your answers to these two questions will guide the structure of your curriculum, selection of your repertoire, your teaching techniques and strategies, as well as how you deal with students and parents.

Once all information is in place, it's time to step out and begin your new career. From your studies in this text you should know what type of independent instruction you'll be embarking upon and what to expect from it.

12.2 Business Set-Up Review

Review the ten steps to setting up an independent music instruction business that are listed here. Upon completion of these steps, your private instruction career can begin.

1. Write a detailed business plan.

Follow the method mapped out in this text to write an original plan.

Obviously, one of the most, if not the most, important aspect of private music education is the income that you will derive from it. Estimating income will confirm several specifics of the business plan.

> *number of lessons to be taught each week*
> x   *price per lesson*
> _____
> **Income possible each week**

Determine how many lessons you will need to teach weekly to make your desired income.

A. Desired Annual Income _____

In-home studio expenses (not including start-up costs)

annual mortgage/rent _____

annual insurance _____

annual phone _____

annual utilities _____

miscellaneous
tunings, repairs _____
printings, ads _____
office supplies _____

incentives/recitals _____

professional services _____

child-care _____

B. Total in-home Expenses _____ *(add Expenses)*

Total Annual Amount Required _____
(total of lines A & B)

The Private Music Instruction Manual: A Guide for the Independent Music Educator • Rebecca Osborn

This exercise will require intelligent conjecture rather than fact. Continue through the next set of figures to set some realistic expectations.

Weeks per academic year   _____
(Don't forget to omit holiday weeks.)

Teaching hours per week   _____ (multiply)

A. **Total hours for academic year**   _____

    Weeks per summer instruction   _____
    (Will you take a vacation?)

    Teaching hours per summer   _____ (multiply)
    (Remember, many students take time off for summer.)

B. **Total hours for summer instruction**   _____

    Total hours for the entire year   _____
                                                  (total of lines A & B)

    Price per hourly lesson   _____ (multiply)

    Total projected annual income   _____

Now compare and contrast the two total figures.

Total Annual Amount Required   _____

Total Projected Annual Income   _____

If there is a huge disparity between these figures, consider any of these three possible solutions:

1. Increase the projected **Lesson Price**
2. Increase the number of weekly lessons taught
3. Decrease the Desired Annual Income

Remember also that your price per lesson must be in keeping with the geographic area in which you are teaching.

2. Finalize an instruction location.

If you have no preference or requirements for your studio location, then analyze the financial variables to aid with this decision.

3. Secure the necessary money for start-up costs.

Make generous estimates of what will be needed to start up and maintain the business for the first six months.

4. Hire the appropriate professionals.

- Attorney-for zoning concerns
- Accountant-for tax guidance and to help secure a tax identity. (It will cost less to hire an accountant for tax advice than a tax attorney.)
- Insurance agent-for liability protection, equipment protection, and for personal needs

5. Purchase any necessary equipment.

Review Chapter 5 of this text for checklists of absolute necessities.

6. Prepare location.

Make any safety, acoustic, and aesthetic preparations necessary for the prospective students and their families.

7. Advertise.

Your teaching philosophy holds the key to the content of your advertising program. Your educational principles coupled with your history will supply the initial text for press releases, advertisements and the studio brochure.

8. Write and print parent guides, policies, and contracts.

Review Chapters 9 and 10 for specifics.

9. Do appropriate and thorough advertising and have a grand opening.

Review some of the advertising ideas presented in Chapter 6 of this text.

The Private Music Instruction Manual: A Guide for the Independent Music Educator • Rebecca Osborn

10. Begin your private teaching career.

Enjoy!

12.2 Budget Your Way to Success

Make a budget for the business. Make a budget for yourself. Music teaching is a seasonal business, and you'll need to learn to budget around the lean times. The school year is the time of greatest financial security in this business. However, you must plan for school vacations since many people will be away and they may stop lessons during these times. Plan for cash flow problems by deciding the percentage which will be banked from September, October, and February. These months are historically the strongest and most financially secure months each year.

It's very easy to financially over-extend. You'll receive many payments in the form of cash. Don't allow the cash in your hand to trick you into thinking there is more money than there actually is. Remember, the majority of small business do not exist long enough to celebrate their second anniversary. Know your budget and stick to it.

Don't be afraid to barter for services. You are supplying a service and perhaps one of your students can supply a service for you in place of monetary payment. Some possible barter examples include:
* snow removal
* house cleaning
* accounting
* child care
* printing
* handy-man service
* screen printing
* tunings and repairs

12.3 Conclusion

From the first moment I began my education career, my greatest joy was getting to know the students and watching them grow. I personally passed through several developmental phases in my teaching. In the beginning, I wanted well-rehearsed and disciplined, competition-winning students. I soon learned that my most important work was helping people, young ones especially, as they found confidence and a new direction in their life journeys.

I have learned that it is easy to underestimate the intelligence and sensitivity of young people. Give your students respect, and ask them to be responsible individuals and to do quality work in a timely fashion. Give them the further respect of doing your job well, and they will respond with mutual respect.

We as music teachers of school-aged students have an advantage over other teachers in that we have better opportunities to communicate with our students. We have the luxury of several years of association as we lay out long-term plans for their musical education. We work with them in social situations, we work with them individually, and we often develop relationships with their families. We have the genuine honor and awesome responsibility of influencing the lives of our students. We have more opportunities for significant influence, and therefore more responsibility than our colleagues in the other disciplines of education.

First, you need to learn to set specific standards for your students. Help them develop work habits that guide them to the understanding necessary as they learn...sometimes in life there will be an inordinate amount of work before you see the reward.

Secondly, don't underestimate your students' abilities to understand and respond to fine music. Don't forget how strong your reactions have been to music, especially when you were young. Most of us were seduced into a career in music and our undying love of its strains during our adolescence. We were hopelessly taken by the power of music as it affected us emotionally.

Thirdly, introduce your students to quality music. Teaching people to value poor music is probably the biggest crime in music education today. Remember, there are two types of music, good and not good. What matters is the quality of the music and not the genre. Good music exists in every genre.

Your studio will not be a success unless you produce and provide results. These results can take many different forms, the greatest of which is changing and influencing the lives of students by introducing them to the innumerable possibilities in music and in life.

You have been given the information, and you now have the tools. Now it's your turn to make the best private music instruction business possible.

APPENDIX A
Practice Log

Practice Log

Name _____

Week of:		Daily Practice times	Day 1	Day 2	Day 3	Day 4	Day 5
Book:	Page:						

Technology Time:

Week of:							
Book:	Page:						

Technology Time:

Week of:							
Book:	Page:						

Technology Time:

Week of:							
Book:	Page:						

Technology Time:

Week of:							
Book:	Page:						

Technology Time:

Week of:							
Book:	Page:						

Technology Time:

APPENDIX B
Publication Release

Studio Name: _____

Owner/Director: _____

Publication Release

I, hereby, for myself, my heirs, executors and administrators, give permission for the free use of my name or my child's name and/or picture in any broadcast, telecast, publication, or other account of the _____ Studio.

Parents/Guardians are asked to sign and date authorization for any child under the age of eighteen.

Signature_____ Date_____

Child_____

APPENDIX C
First Chair Flyer

APPENDIX D
Composer of the Month

Composer of the Month
Birthdays

January 4, 1710 .... Pergolesi, Giovanni Battista
Januray 7, 1899 .... Poulenc, Francis
January 23, 1752 .... Clementi, Muzio
January 27, 1756 .... Mozart, Wolfgang Amadeus
January 31, 1797 .... Schubert, Franz Peter
February 3, 1809 .... Mendelssohn, Jacob Felix
February 20, 1791 .... Czerny, Carl
February 23, 1685 .... Handel, George Frederic
February 25, 1727 ....Couperin, Armand-Louis
February 29, 1792 ....Rossini, Gioachino Antonio
March 1, 1810 ....Chopin, Frederic
March 4, 1678 ....Vivaldi, Antonio
March 8, 1714 .... Bach, Carl Philipp Emanuel
March 9, 1920 .... Barber, Samuel
March 18, 1844 ....Rimsky-Korsakov, Nikolai
March 21, 1685 .... Bach, Johann Sebastian
March 31, 1732 ....Haydn, Franz Joseph
April 1, 1873 ....Rachmaninov, Sergei
April 27, 1891 .... Prokofiev, Sergei
May 2, 1660 ....Scarlatti, Alessandro
May 7, 1833 .... Brahms, Johannes
May 7, 1840 .... Tchaikovsky, Pyotr Il'yich
June 15, 1843 ....Grieg, Edvard
July 2, 1714 ....Gluck, Christoph
August 22, 1862 .... Debussy, Claude
August 25, 1918 .... Bernstein, Leonard
September 9, 1841 .... Dvořák, Antonín
September 11, 1786 ....Kuhlau, Friedrich
September 21, 1874 .... Holst, Gustav
September 26, 1898 .... Gershwin, George
October 9, 1835 ....Saint-Saëns, Charles-Camille
October 20, 1874 ....Ives, Charles
October 22, 1811 .... Liszt, Franz
November 6, 1854 ....Sousa, John Phillip
November 14, 1900 ....Copland, Aaron
December 8, 1865 ....Sibelius, Jean
December 15, 1770 .... Beethoven, Ludwig van
December 16, 1882 ....Kodály, Zoltán

APPENDIX E
Studio Brochure

MUSIC of OZ

s t u d i o

Offering
professional training
in all musical interests

piano	trombone
voice	baritone
flute	tuba
oboe	violin
clarinet	viola
saxophone	cello
French horn	double bass
cornet	guitar
trumpet	bass guitar

PAYMENT POLICY

Private music lessons at Music of Oz Studio cost $50.00 tuition per month for voice, wind, and piano lessons. All string lessons cost $56.00 each month. This will cover four or five weekly sessions; the charge remains the same per month regardless of the number of lesson days appearing on the calendar. This fee must be paid at the student's first lesson of each month.

Student cancellations will be rescheduled whenever possible. Twenty-four hours notice is appreciated. Students will be given one month to make up a missed lesson. If it is not rescheduled by the end of the month, no reimbursement or credit will be given. Students are encouraged to trade lesson times rather than cancel if at all possible. Students will be billed for no call or no show lessons. In the event that Music of Oz Studio must cancel a lesson (holiday, illness, *etc.*), your account will be credited.

WELCOME TO
Music of Oz Studio

Music of Oz Studio is a professional music studio specializing in private music studies. Music of Oz Studio offers instruction in piano, voice, wind, and string instruments.

A staff of talented, trained, and accomplished educators join studio director Rebecca Osborn. They provide quality specialized musical instruction to students of all ages and ability levels.

At Music of Oz Studio, instructors understand the differing needs and goals of individual students and adjust and personalize curricula accordingly. Whether seeking fame and fortune, a career in music, or simply pursuing a few hours of fun at home, students ages seven through adult at all levels of proficiency are encouraged at Music of Oz Studio.

MEET THE DIRECTOR

Becky Osborn has spent her adult life as a music educator. A graduate of Butler University Jordan College of Music with a degree in music education, she also has a Master of Liberal Arts and Science degree from Valparaiso University. She taught high school choral music for sixteen years and left public education to follow other musical pursuits. She is the founder and director of the Kankakee Valley Community Choir, an adult Christian choir, and is very active in community theatre as well.

Recognizing the need for a studio which offers expert musical instruction and is locally convenient, Becky founded the Music of Oz Studio.

Becky's teaching style makes lessons fun, as well as educational. She also works at encouraging students both personally and musically. She has passed her approach to music education on to her staff at Music of Oz Studio.

ABOUT THE STUDIO

Music of OZ Studio features recital programs and special awards. Students are encouraged to participate in ISSMA and Junior Music Festival Federation solo and ensemble contests. All staff members use our incentive plan featuring "Oz Bucks," which can be redeemed for merchandise or gift certificates.

Music of Oz Studio is located at 614 Second Avenue NW in DeMotte, IN. To find us easily, please walk around to the back entrance.

Office Phone: 219.987.7161

FURTHER INFORMATION

The studio will be closed on Memorial Day, July 4th, Labor Day, Thanksgiving weekend, and the week between Christmas and New Year's Day.

Remember, adults are welcome and encouraged!

Know someone who'd like to try music lessons?

Gift certificates are available.

APPENDIX F
Studio Festival Sign-up and Fees

The _____ Studio Festival
Music Teachers National Association
Studio Festival Program

Date: _____

Subject: Studio Festival

Important Notice to: _____

Parents/Guardian of: _____

Festival Date:_____   Location:_____

The _____ Studio firmly believes that quality teaching is enhanced by performance opportunities and positive reinforcement of outside professional musicians. As such, the _____ Studio is sponsoring their annual Festival in which students are evaluated and given the opportunity to earn ribbons, certificates, and trophies.

This program requires considerable advance planning. Please complete the form below and return at the student's next lesson. Student's performance times will be posted at the studio 10-14 days before the festival.

Please sign and return with entry fees no later than March 15th.

- -

Student's Name_____ Teacher_____

_____ Will participate in the Studio Festival this year.

_____ A special performance time is needed. (The studio will make every effort to honor special time requests)

_____ Will not participate in the Studio Festival this year.

If participating, please send Studio Festival fee with this form. The cost of each event is $7.00.

_____ Events @ $7.00 each. List each event:

$_____ Total Fee

Fees are non-refundable.
Make checks payable to The Studio Festival.

APPENDIX G
Games & Activities

Games and Activities to Teach the Elements

Finger Numbers (keyboard and string instruments)

Materials: dry erase board and pen
or paper and pen

One hand starts out in position. The teacher writes 3 finger numbers on the board. The student plays using the 3 finger numbers listed on one hand. The teacher then erases the pattern and the student plays it back accurately. If they play it correctly they get a point. It they play it incorrectly, the teacher gets a point. As the student gets better, increase the level of difficulty.

If the student is in danger of losing, make the last example a 3 pointer you know the student is capable of. This way, the teacher will never win. Students get so excited about the fact that they were able to beat the teacher.

Melody Memory

Materials: note cards with staff and notes (8 pair)
any instrument

Shuffle the cards and lay them face down and play a regular memory game. When the student finds a match, they should name the note and play it on their instrument. If the student does not match or misplays the note then the teacher gets the point. If the teacher gets a match, the student can steal the point by naming the playing the note before the teacher.

Once again, this is an easily "fixed" activity that the student should always win.

Making Melodies

Materials: chalk board, chalk
or dry erase and markers
Cards with note names, (one for each note)
Cards with note values (can either have the name of note or a picture, depending on the ability level of the class)of whole, half, quarter, and eighth.

Draw large staff on board with treble clef and 4/4 time signature. Place bar lines on the board making 5 measures.

Have students draw a letter name card and a note value card. Go to the board and draw a note on the appropriate line in any measure. They continue realizing that each measure should eventually have 4 beats in it. Have the student clap the rhythm of this melody. Play the melody on a melody instrument or sing it for further closure. The student could even write lyrics for further development as an assignment for the future.

Beanie Baby Note I.D.

Materials: Beanie Baby for each letter of the musical alphabet
staff on floor with black ropes or electric tape

Student reaches into a bag and gets beanie baby. The student takes it and puts in on the staff in the correct position of the line or space which is the beginning letter of the name of the beanie. When all babies are in place start all over again.

Variation: Make draw pile that says, line note or space note.

Phone Number Melodies

A melody is a tune we hear when we listen to a song. When you dial a number on a push button telephone you hear a melody.

0	1	2	3	4	5	6	7	8	9
C	C	D	E	F	G	A	B	C	C

Each number represents a note of the scale. Using this code, figure out the melody of these phone numbers:

464-0123
911-2000
555-4197

Now try your own phone number.

Now experiment with rhythms.
- Let all numbers be quarter notes.
- Let all numbers be half notes.
- Let the numbers be a combination of the two and take up 4 measures of 4/4 time.

Dynamic Dice Drumming

Materials: big die
dry erase board and marker
or chalk board

Key: 1=*pp*, 2=*mp*, 3=*mf*, 4=*ff*, 5= $<$, and 6= $>$

Write a rhythm on the board that is assigned to each number 1-6. Rhythms will be at whatever difficulty level the student is able to perform.

The student will roll the die and perform the rhythm assigned to the number. The student will roll again to find what dynamic level that will be performed (each number is also assigned a dynamic, see Key above). The student will then perform the appropriate rhythm at the appropriate dynamic level on their instrument of study.

Musical Snacks

Materials: 1 can of cheese (such as Easy Cheese)
crackers
musical math note equation cards

Give the student a cracker.

Have the student pick a card. They must do the musical math problem in their head. In order to answer, the student must draw the proper note on the cracker.

Upon completion, the student may eat their cracker.

APPENDIX H
Sample Recital Certificate

CERTIFICATE
of
PERFORMANCE

This is to certify that

_____

has successfully performed in recital on the date of

_____

MUSIC
OF OZ
s t u d i o

_____
Rebecca C. Osborn, Owner/Director

_____
Private Instructor

APPENDIX I
Recital Timeline Checklist

Recital Timeline Checklist

One month before the recital:

☐ Prepare recital sign-up sheets.

☐ Put announcements on dry erase boards, put up signs, do any of the visual advertising your studio usually does to announce/remind of the recital date, time, participants, and location.

Two weeks before the recital:

☐ Put up food sign-up sheets and encourage people to sign up to bring finger food. Let them know what the studio supplies.

☐ Recruit program distributers.

☐ Recruit parents for photography.

☐ Recruit clean-up crew for post recital.

☐ Complete recital sign-up sheet.

☐ Send a mass email to students announcing/reminding of the recital.

☐ Post the "bow signs."

☐ Be knowledgable about what's happening, know the directions to the location, have maps available; if students need information on paper...give it to them.

One week before the recital:

☐ Post the program prototype so additions and corrections can be made.

☐ Type the program for your studio.

☐ Run and fold the programs at least two days prior to the recital.

Come to the recital:

☐ Introduce, welcome, and start the recital. It's your big moment of public speaking!

The week after the recital:

☐ Send a thank you note to helpful parents.

☐ Send a thank you note and a gift to the sound person.

☐ Write a press release and send it to local press regarding the recital. Use any pictures that are available.

APPENDIX J
Deductions

DEDUCTIONS: Expenses & Income

Expense Categories

Advertisement
- Print
- Radio
- Television

Auto
- Fuel
- Service
- Mileage

Awards/Incentives

Bank Charges

Carpet Cleaning

Charity/Donation

Child Care

Cleaning Service

Clothing

Computer Hardware/
Software

Cost of Goods
- Labor
- Materials

Depreciation
- House
- Instrument(s)
- Equipment

Dues for professional
organizations

Education

Entertainment
- Dining
- Lodging
- Shows
- Travel

Equipment
- Instrument(s)
- Piano
- Computer
- Copier

Flooring

Furniture

Gifts

Improvements

Insurance
- Home/studio property
- Health/disability
- Auto
- Liability

Instruments

Interest Paid

Legal Fees

Mortgage

Music
- Scores
- Books
- Recordings

Office Supplies

Pension

Piano Tuning

Postage

Printing

Professional Fees
- Accountant
- Attorney
- Insurance Broker

Public Relations

Recital
- Refreshments
- Facility
- Staff

Refund

Rent Paid

Repairs

Retirement Plan

Services
- Yard
- Snow removal
- Janitorial
- Equipment repair

Subscriptions

Supplies Miscellaneous

Taxes
- Income/self-employment
- Property
- Sales
- Other

Telephone

Travel
- Air/ground
- Meals/lodging

Utilities
- Gas & Electric
- Water

Website
- Design
- Hosting
- Maintenance

Others

Income Categories

Bank Dividend
Gifts Received
Interest Earned
Salary/Wage

APPENDIX K
Floor Plan

Example Home Floor Plan: In-Home Studio Space

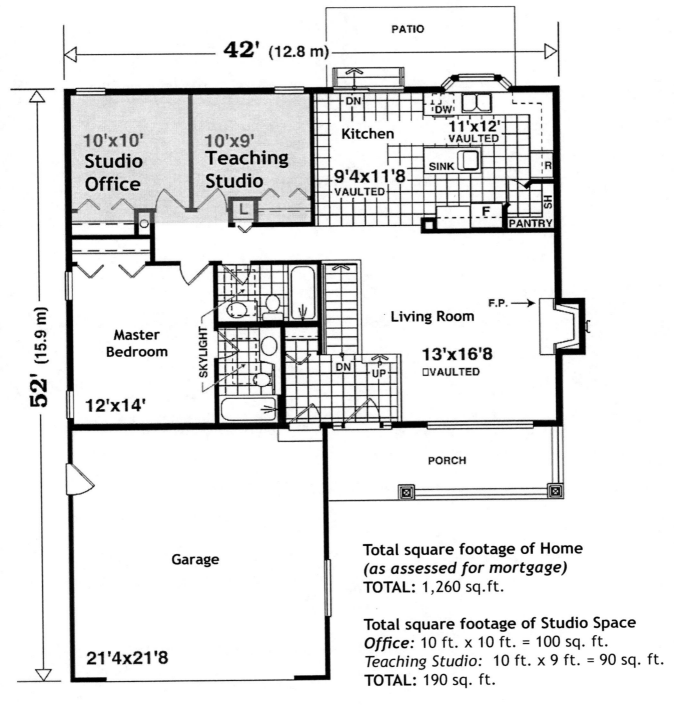

42' (12.8 m)

52' (15.9 m)

PATIO

DN

Kitchen

DW

11'x12'
VAULTED

SINK

9'4x11'8
VAULTED

R

SH

F

PANTRY

10'x10'
Studio
Office

10'x9'
Teaching
Studio

L

Master
Bedroom

12'x14'

SKYLIGHT

DN

UP

Living Room

F.P.

13'x16'8
◻VAULTED

Garage

21'4x21'8

PORCH

Total square footage of Home
(as assessed for mortgage)
TOTAL: 1,260 sq.ft.

Total square footage of Studio Space
Office: 10 ft. x 10 ft. = 100 sq. ft.
Teaching Studio: 10 ft. x 9 ft. = 90 sq. ft.
TOTAL: 190 sq. ft.

Percentage of Home used as Studio
190 / 1,260 = 15%

APPENDIX L
Collection Letters

PAST DUE NOTICE #1

Dear _____,   Date _____

Just a friendly reminder that your tuition has not been paid for the month of _____.
You may mail your check to me today, or bring it in to the studio.

The amount due is $_____.

For future reference, please be aware that tuition is always due the first lesson of
each month. Please refer to your copy of the Payment Policy Agreement. As per this
agreement, a late fee has been applied to your bill.

If you have any question regarding this bill, please feel free to contact me at _____.

Sincerely,

PAST DUE NOTICE #2

Dear _____,   Date _____

May I call your attention to your tuition payment that you have no doubt overlooked?
It is 30 days past due. As per the Payment Policy Agreement which you signed, lessons
will be suspended and your lesson time will be forfeited if I don't receive payment
immediately.

The amount due is $_____ which includes a $_____ late fee.

If you have any question regarding this bill, please feel free to contact me at _____.

Sincerely,

PAST DUE NOTICE #3

Dear _____,   Date_____

There must be a reason why I haven't heard from you after our two previous written reminders. Will you let me know why?

Since I know you wish to pay your bills when they are due, I expect that these overdue tuitions are just an oversight on your part.

As you know, my studio policy prohibits extending credit to customers who have outstanding past due charges. I will have no alternative but to seek legal action.

Your tuition balance which is past due is: $ _____

The enclosed self-addressed envelope is for your convenience. If I can be of any help to you in this matter, please feel free to call me at this number, _____.

Sincerely,

APPENDIX M
Parent Guide:
Beginning Students

Successful Home Practice

Music of Oz Studio
PRIVATE INSTRUCTION
Parent Guide Series

INTRODUCTION

Now that your son or daughter has some experience as a beginning musician, the following information has been compiled as a guide for parents to help monitor progress. By now, your child has been taught proper posture, the method of producing a tone, and several different songs.

HOME REVIEW

One excellent method of reinforcing what has been taught during private lessons, is to ask your child to teach someone else. Using yourself or a brother or sister, ask your child to teach one of the beginning songs that they have learned. This way, your child will be able to review the basics needed for their own performing. This will also help to build your child's confidence.

HOME PRACTICE

Home practice is handled differently in every household. Parents are often hesitant to "force" their children to practice, but children MUST practice daily in order for progress to occur. Consistent daily practice is the ONLY way a student can be successful in music in the long term.

The following guidelines provide basic information regarding practice expectations. While some of these points might seem elementary, it is much more difficult to break bad habits than it is to create new ones. Please go over these guidelines with your child now and throughout the year to help ensure their success.

1. Establish a regular 30-minute daily period when your child can concentrate on practicing. It is far more beneficial for a student to practice for 30 minutes each day than it is for a student to practice for longer periods in fewer days.

2. Proper posture and/or instrument position is essential for producing a good sound and proficiency on any musical medium. Vocal and instrumental students should sit up straight in a chair with both feet flat on the floor. A vocalist may also prefer to stand. Piano students should sit a comfortable distance from the keyboard with curved fingers, high wrists, and a straight back. Music should be placed at eye level.

3. When practicing, students should not just be playing or singing through the notes. Time should be taken to COUNT and CLAP rhythms, review fingering or positions of each note, check breathing and mouth and tongue position, and read letter names of notes aloud. When playing, the goal is to play or sing without stumbling or "stuttering" over notes. When a problem area is encountered, the problem should be practiced several times until it is played smoothly and then return to the beginning of the line and try the entire line again.

4. The tone quality of beginning students will undoubtedly be unrefined. However, the sound should be full and solid, but NEVER forced, blasted, pushed, or banged.

5. Toward the end of a practice session, it is advisable for students to go back and play previous accomplishments or favorite songs. This serves as both an excellent review and a reward for their practice time.

6. Each instrument needs special care. At the end of each playing session, instruments should be put back in their case for safe storage. Proper cleaning and storage will keep the instrument in good playing order, as well as help to retain its value. (Specific maintenance techniques for each instrument are discussed by each teacher.) Vocalists should learn to treat their body as their instrument, always drinking plenty of WATER after a practice session. Pianos should be closed so they can remain free of dust and dirt.

THANK YOU

Thank you for your help and support during the beginning stages of your child's musical development. Please feel free to ask any questions of any staff members, and remember that we are all here for the benefit of YOUR child.

Sincerely,

APPENDIX N
Parent Guide: Beginning Piano Students

Parent Guide for Piano Students

INTRODUCTION

Parents who do not read music or play the piano themselves can still provide their children with the two most important ingredients needed for their child's musical success: Support & Encouragement.

PRACTICE LOGS

Each child is given a practice log to record weekly assignments. On this, the teacher will write specific page numbers, song titles, and the number of times a song should be run through each day. Students receive a stamp or sticker on their sheet if a week's practice is successfully completed. They will place their name in the weekly legato lotto drawing at the end of a successful week of practice. Six successful practice weeks will be rewarded with one Oz Buck.

STUDENT CHECKLIST

1. Wash hands.
2. Play warm-up exercises.
3. Play assigned pieces.
4. Mark off success on the practice log.
5. Play through "old favorites" as a reward at the end of practice.

VARY YOUR PRACTICE

- Try practicing the whole song f (LOUD).
- Try practicing the whole song p (soft).
- Try practicing the whole song s t a c a t t o.
- Try practicing the whole song **legato.**
- Try practicing the whole song in a ^higher^ or ₗₒwₑᵣ octave (8va)

PARENT PRELIMINARIES

1. Schedule practicing for a time when your child is not too tired.
2. Schedule practice close to the same time each day so that music becomes a part of the child's life and routine.
3. Provide a snack before practice.
4. Keep distractions (TV, siblings, *etc.*) to a minimum during practice time.
5. Provide adequate lighting at the piano.
6. Remind piano players to keep fingernails short.

PARENT CHECKLIST

1. Sit next to your child at practice.
2. Check that fingers are curved and near the black keys.
3. Make sure bench is close enough for relaxed arm position and child is sitting toward the back of the bench with knees under the piano.
4. Several of the songs have lyrics. Sing along and encourage the child to do the same. (When they hear how the words move along, they'll be less likely to hesitate within the song.)
5. Occasionally move back from the child to see if any part of the body is tense. When the body is balanced, relaxation is more easily attained.
6. End the practice by listening to your child play his/her favorite piece (old or new).

Check out the handy-dandy help chart for quick piano technique guidelines.

HELP CHART: Terms and Meanings

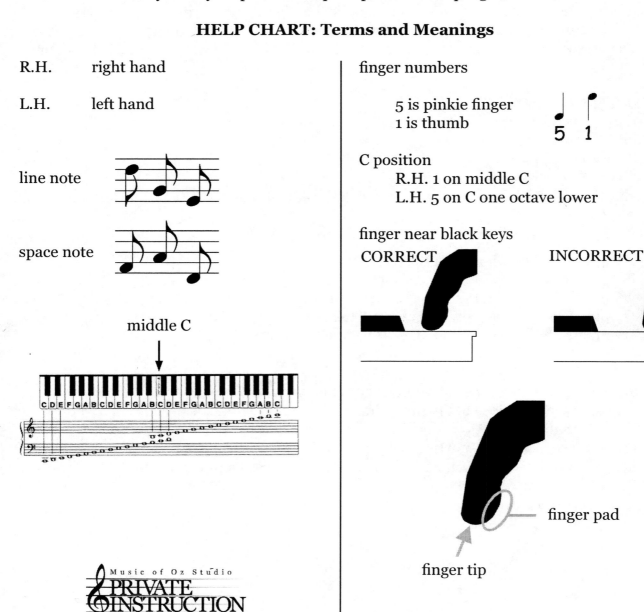

R.H.   right hand

L.H.   left hand

line note

space note

middle C

finger numbers

    5 is pinkie finger
    1 is thumb

    5   1

C position
    R.H. 1 on middle C
    L.H. 5 on C one octave lower

finger near black keys
CORRECT   INCORRECT

finger pad

finger tip

Music of Oz Studio
PRIVATE
INSTRUCTION
Parent Guide Series

APPENDIX O
Parent Guide: Beginning Voice Students

Parent Guide for Voice Students

Music of Oz Studio
PRIVATE INSTRUCTION
Parent Guide Series

INTRODUCTION

We here at the _____ Studios want to answer any questions concerning the need for vocal studies. After all, we were all born with a voice and we use it every day, so why the need for training in something we already know how to use?

BACKGROUND INFORMATION

Singing is like any other physical activity. It uses muscles. Just as you must learn to stretch and control muscles for any sport, you must also learn to stretch and control the vocal muscles for singing. Vocal music instruction will teach proper muscle use including, diaphragm and rib control for proper breathing, as well as proper tongue and mouth position for vowel and consonant formation. Physical damage can occur from improper use of singing muscles. Prolonged "school-bus singing" can permanently damage the vocal cords.

LESSON BASICS

Each lesson will include work on musical information and technique such as:
- intonation-ear/pitch control-flatting or sharping.
- breathing.
- diction and articulation.
- note accuracy.

If a student is to be judged by note accuracy, it is essential that a student read notes. Though it is acceptable in some cases to sing songs by imitation, it is important to learn to read music. This will allow the student to read and accurately sing the notes written in the music.

REPERTOIRE

The Studios help a student improve and increase their repertoire by offering many types of musical selections in the students' interest area, as well as basic "teaching" songs. Attention to musical detail will be stressed. This will include:
- interpretation and musicianship.
- dynamics and phrasing.
- tempo, expression, and style.

STAGE PRESENTATION

It is very important to understand the different presentation required by each type of vocal music, from a church solo to a talent show. A student with innate musical ability doesn't always posses innate stage presence. This must be taught and learned through performance. The Studio offers many opportunities for student performances through recitals, repertoire classes, contests and festivals. These performance opportunities will teach stage presence through: appearance, posture, and message.

STUDENT CHECKLIST

1. Students will need to supply their own folders (preferably a 3-ring binder) to keep their musical library.
2. A tape will be provided and accompaniments and warm-ups will be taped for each student.
3. Each student will be given a practice log with weekly assignments.
4. Worksheets and music theory workbooks will be used as supplemental materials.

These materials should be brought to each lesson with the student.

PARENT CHECKLIST

1. Schedule practicing for a time when your child is not too tired.
2. Schedule practice close to the same time each day so that music becomes a part of the child's life and daily routine.
3. Encourage your child to have a snack after practice and not before.
4, Keep distractions (TV, siblings, *etc.*) to a minimum during practice time.
5. Check to make sure your child brings all their materials to their lesson.
6. Encourage and support your child by allowing them to take part in performing opportunities.
7. Feel free to ask questions.

APPENDIX P
Piano Student Inventory

Piano Student Inventory

Student Name_____ Age_____

School_____ Grade_____

Musical Background:_____

_____

Performing Experience:_____

_____

Current Series:_____

Assessment

Hand Position:_____

Scales: Representative Keys_____

              One or Two Octaves_____

              Representative Literature:_____

              _____

General Musicianship: _____

          Phrasing:_____   Pedaling:_____

          Technique:_____   Dynamics:_____

          Sightreading:_____   Note Recognition:_____

          Keys:_____   Rhythmic Awareness:_____

Transposing:_____

Chords/Fake Book Knowledge:_____

Goals and Desire:_____

Personality Description:_____

APPENDIX Q
Voice Student Inventory

Voice Student Inventory

Student Name_____ Age_____

School_____ Grade_____

Musical Background:_____

_____

Representative Listening:_____

Performing Experience:_____

_____

Assessment

Range:_____ Breaks:_____

Representative Literature:_____

_____

General Musicianship:_____

    Phrasing:_____ Breathing:_____

    Quality:_____ Pitch:_____

Sightreading:_____

    Keys:_____ Rhythmic Awareness:_____

    Solfege:_____ Symbols:_____

    Pitch Retention:_____

    Ability to Improvise:_____

Personality Description:_____

Desire:_____

INDEX

ISBN 1-4120-2531-1